# GIRL GONE GLAD

A memoir of self-discovery, awareness, and the truth
about how narcissistic abuse survivors can find joy,
peace, and love!

---

## SHARON LEE VILLONE

Internet addresses given in this book were accurate at the time it went to press.

This book is intended as a reference volume only, not as a medical manual. The information given here is based on the author's opinion and perception of personal experiences. Names have been changed to protect the privacy of those involved. This book is designed to inspire, inform, and motivate. It is not intended as a substitute for any treatment that may have been prescribed by your doctor. If you suspect that you are being abused, we urge you to seek professional help.

Printed in the United States of America

Published in Hellertown, PA

Cover design by Sharon Lee Villone

Library of Congress Control Number 2023911441

ISBN 978-1-958711-57-6

For more information or to place bulk orders, contact the author or the publisher at Jennifer@BrightCommunications.net.

# Contents

*To my children, Samantha and Nicholas: Your love and support have carried me through my most challenging days. I am so proud of the strong, independent, and moral individuals you have become and grateful for your friendship.*

*To my grandchildren, Makynli and Lennon: Your love, laughter, innocence, and curiosity fill my cup every day. Nothing makes me happier than watching you learn and grow.*

*To the victims of narcissistic abuse: You can find the love and respect that you absolutely deserve. Stay strong, be patient, and trust the process!*

# "The Best"

## CONFESSIONS OF A NARCISSIST

You're THE BEST.

The one I've been searching for.

I've never met anyone like you.

I feel so good when I'm near you.

You are amazing.

I want to be with you—always.

I need you.

All of you.

Your time and attention.

Your loyalty and devotion.

Your kind heart and trusting soul.

You sustain me.

I love you, and I want you to love me too.

I need you to believe in me so I'll tell you what you want to hear until you trust me.

I'll be who you want me to be until you invest in me.

I'll be your everything, your one true love, your soulmate.

And you'll be mine.

So talk to me.

Confide in me your fears and insecurities.

Tell me your deepest, darkest secrets.

After all, I have mine too.

But you'll never know them.

Until it's too late.

Don't worry, I'm here for you.

Unlike anyone else.

You'll see.

And when you do, you'll be mine.

All mine.

I'll own you.

And I'll use you.

Like I use everything that is mine.

But everything gets old when the newness wears away.

You will too.

In my eyes, you'll change, simply by being you.

The same you who I adored.

Your vibrancy will dissipate.

And your presence will no longer thrill me.

You'll lose your effect on me

There's nothing you can do about it.

This is unacceptable.

Damn you.

How dare you do this to me.

After all I've done for you.

I worshipped you.

You'll pay a price for this.

I'll make sure of it.

Remember those fears?

Those insecurities?

I'll use them against you.

I remember them all.

And I won't let you forget them.

Your wounds will never heal as long as I'm around.

I'll see to that.

But don't worry, I'll stand by you.

You should be grateful because I'm so much better than you.

I'll help you.

I'll build you up higher than before.

You'll see.

And just when you think all is well.

Just when you're getting comfortable and feeling good about you and us again.

I'll set you up for the fall.

I have to.

Because the further you fall, the better I feel—for a little while anyway.

And the tears you shed?

They're delightful.

Merely evidence of my power over you.

Look at you.

You're so weak.

Nothing like the person I knew when we met.

You were appealing then.

And strong.

I deserve so much better than what you have become.

But regardless of your shortcomings, I'll be here for you.

Until you need me.

I'll tell you I love you, knowing my actions will never match my words.

My love is conditional.

I'll promise you everything and deliver nothing.

I'll keep you hanging on a hope and a dream.

I'll cast you into purgatory and make you believe it's your fault.

It's a pleasure to watch as you spin in circles trying to please me.

So that I might return you to your pedestal.

It was a wonderful place to be, wasn't it?

Don't worry.

I'll put you back.

In due time.

Anything for you.

I can play this game forever.

I thoroughly enjoy a rollercoaster ride.

The ups and downs are exhilarating.

How satisfying it is to control you.

And consume your thoughts.

Happy one minute, sad the next, with just a single word or glance.

This is far too easy.

The power I have over you is intoxicating.

And pathetic.

Only a fool would accept this type of treatment.

You're despicable.

I'm worthy of someone amazing.

Like myself.

You were amazing once.

What happened to you?

You don't expect me to continue like this, do you?

Don't you know who I am?

I won't stop until I find what I am looking for.

And when I do, we'll be finished.

Because I deserve nothing but THE BEST.

# Author's Note

At some point, every target of narcissistic abuse will ask themselves, "Is it me? Is it my fault that this relationship isn't working?" Confusion and uncertainty are common threads among victims who will take responsibility for an abusive relationship in an attempt to keep the peace and stop the madness that is consuming their lives. Self-doubt and self-blame are among the symptoms that manifest from the psychological abuse of a narcissist.

Over the past four years, I have spoken to more than 500 survivors seeking relief from the agony inflicted by a narcissistic loved one and eager to speak with others who can relate. Their road to recovery is long and arduous with many setbacks, but the rewards at the end of their journeys couldn't be sweeter. For far too long, narcissism has taken a comfortable seat in a dark corner of our society while quietly destroying lives.

Someone with Narcissistic Personality Disorder will target unsuspecting victims, including spouses, family members, boyfriends/girlfriends, friends, etc., who become sources of supply for the insatiable, attention-seeking narcissist. Using psychological manipulation, a narcissist will attempt to make their victims feel stupid, crazy, weak, worthless, useless, incapable, incompetent, undesirable, unworthy, and unloveable. The target of a narcissist's abuse will eventually feel like they are not good enough, resulting in an unhealthy need to please and appease by loving more, doing more, giving more, or providing more.

Due to the insidiousness of the abuse, victims can go for years, decades, or a lifetime without realizing that they are being abused; all the while suffering from a multitude of mental, emotional, and physical ailments.

Narcissists are cunning and deceitful. They will smile to your face, stab you in the back, and laugh while you bleed. They cannot love in the true sense of the word and have little to no empathy. They are takers who gain full control in relationships by manipulating other people to fulfill their own wants and needs. To them, nothing else matters. To get attention, a narcissist will be the loudest one in the room or the poor victim quietly sulking in the corner. Narcissists can be extremely boastful about their accomplishments, regardless of how big or small, or they can act as the innocent, wounded party by blaming other people for their setbacks and shortcomings. Either way, the result is the same: attention and control.

Narcissistic abuse can be devastating to your self-worth, but rest assured that with the proper information and guidance, there is a light at the end of the tunnel.

This book, delivered with humor and wit, is a personal account based solely on my opinion, perspective, and recol-

lection of my experiences. It is in no way intended to
diminish the harmful effects of narcissistic abuse but rather
to raise awareness and give hope to other sufferers. The
male pronouns that I use are based on my personal experience with male abusers and in no way imply that all narcissists are male.

I am a midlife, single, narcissistic abuse survivor, and these
are the revelations that healed me.

Love is patient, Love is kind.
It does not envy, it does not boast, it is not proud.
It does not dishonor others, it is not self-seeking,
it is not easily angered, it keeps no record of wrongs.
Love does not delight in evil but rejoices with the truth.
It always protects, always trusts, always hopes, always
perseveres.
Love never fails.
1 Corinthians 13: 4-8

"Somewhere between what she survived,
and who she was becoming,
was exactly where she was meant to be.
She was starting to love the journey."
—J. Raymond

# Preface

Love.

Hats off to those who have found it, kept it, and shout it from the rooftops or on the pages of Facebook, Instagram, and other social media outlets with romantic photos and kissy face emojis. For me, the search for love can seem futile at times. Of course, with age comes wisdom and a higher level of maturity, so I have a clearer idea of what I am looking for in a potential partner. But certainly one of the biggest challenges of being midlife and single is dating. And with midlife dating comes a whole lot of baggage!

At this age, we've all accumulated it. Let's face it: If all our baggage doesn't fit into the overhead, the "plane" is most likely never getting off the ground. The obvious, most commonsense thing to do in this instance is to get off the plane. However, no one knows better than I do, that it is much easier said than done, especially if it's a plane with awesome amenities and a destination point that promises to be even better!

Many of us have tried to make the baggage fit. We've moved it around, twisted and turned it, sat on it to squash it down a little; repacked, re-zipped, and crammed it into a space where it does not belong just so the plane will take off. The flight is smooth for a little while, and in spite of the bulging compartment overhead, we manage to be lulled into a false sense of comfort and security until *wham*! Before the plane reaches full altitude, the overhead bin flies open, and the baggage spills out into the cabin. The contents of the baggage pose a real threat to the plane, so to avoid serious consequences, the flight is diverted.

Unfortunately, a plane can't stop in midair and let us and our baggage out. Procedures and protocol have to be followed for the plane to turn around and land safely, so no matter how turbulent the air is on the way back, we are in for the ride! It tosses us around, up and down, side to side, until we land and exit with unsteady footing and a reluctance to ever fly again! But we usually do.

Like the anxiety we feel after a turbulent plane ride, we take emotional hits from failed marriages and relationships that can lead to a real hesitance to ever love or trust again. Some emotional wounds heal quicker than others, and the scars that remain can be a constant reminder that the end of a long-term relationship can bring us to our knees. It can be paralyzing, devastating, and debilitating. It can feel scary, hopeless, and lonely. The end of a relationship can be one of the most difficult things we've ever gone through as we ponder some very difficult questions:

*What do I do now?*

*How do I start over?*

*Can I make it on my own?*

A breakup can leave us in the throes of depression as we are forced to let go of the past and our dreams of what could have or should have been. In some cases, the end of a relationship, no matter how turbulent or toxic, can lead us to a place where we never thought we would be, as it did me.

I am a Girl Gone Glad!

# The Truth, the Whole Truth

## AND NOTHING BUT THE TRUTH

*To know thyself is the greatest gift you can give yourself.*

Being single is definitely *not* where I thought I would be at this stage of my life. To be honest, my midlife dating experiences could more than fill the pages of this book, but this is not *that* kind of story. This is a story about love and how this phase of my life has opened my eyes to how much I didn't know about it.

If your experiences have led you to a healthy, loving relationship with a life partner, congratulations! But if like me, you have struggled in the love department, you know exactly what I am talking about. Over the past few years, I have been dedicated to figuring it out—I mean, figuring *me* out. I am smart enough to know that the solution to any problem begins with the truth, which until recently, I thought I was pretty good at.

I was raised in a home where meatloaf and mashed pota-
toes were served with a side of guilt to keep me honest and
on the right track. I was taught to treat others as I would
like to be treated. So I did. I was taught that in giving I shall
receive. So I gave. And I was taught to always tell the truth.
So I did.

At least I thought I did. But as it turned out, I wasn't
truthful at all. As a matter of fact, my first revelation of
being a midlife single was discovering that I was a big, fat,
liar, who lied a lot to the one person who matters most: me.
And, in doing so, I lied to others I claimed to love. I lied
about what I wanted and needed because I felt guilty for
having wants and needs at all. Actually, I had no idea what
my wants and needs even were!

I thought love was all about giving. In every relationship, I
gave to satisfy the other person. It felt good thinking that I
was making someone else happy by meeting their needs. My
own happiness was irrelevant.

I delighted in my ability to morph into the role of what
someone else wanted me to be. It was like a drug that satis-
fied an underlying craving to please.

Therefore, who was I most drawn to? People who wanted to
be pleased, of course. I was naturally attracted to partners
who had little to no regard for *my* thoughts or feelings.
There couldn't be a more dangerous match for a people-
pleaser than someone with an insatiable, unsatisfied appetite
for attention, aka, a narcissist. A relationship between a
people-pleaser and a narcissist is a perfect storm; a toxic
dance between a giver and a taker.

These relationships are like any other unhealthy addiction where the highs are amazing and the lows are detrimental. Over the years, I have identified several relationships in my life as such. Although there were distinct differences in each one, I found myself posing the same questions:

*Why does he act like that?*

*Why would he say that?*

*Why does he treat me like that?*

In each relationship, the person I was with changed for the worse as the relationship deepened. I spent most of my time wondering why I didn't *feel* loved and why someone who claimed to love me didn't *act* loving. I wanted to figure out what I could say or do to make each partner change back into the person I had initially fallen in love with so we could have the healthy, loving relationship that I knew was possible. I asked myself:

*How can I make him "get it?"*

*What can I say to make him understand?*

*How can I explain things differently to make him change so that this will work?*

When I wasn't torturing myself with questions, I agonized over the if only's:

*If only he would listen to me.*

*If only he would understand how I feel.*

*If only he wouldn't get annoyed or angry when I try talking to him.*

*If only he would stop blaming me for everything.*

*If only he would stop ignoring me.*

*If only he would stop belittling me.*

*If only he would stop criticizing me.*

*If only he would stop lying to me.*

*If only, if only, if only!*

My frustration level was akin to Cinderella's stepsisters trying to squeeze their big feet into that tiny, little slipper. They kept pushing and readjusting to push some more, but the slipper was made of glass so it didn't budge! It took several relationships and decades of pushing and readjusting to accept the fact that I can't change anyone! With this revelation, I began asking myself different questions:

*Why do I feel the same in this relationship as I felt in the past one?*

*Why have I allowed myself to be treated so poorly?*

*What role am I playing in these toxic relationships?*

*Am I part of the dysfunction?*

Talk about opening up a can of worms! Once I began asking myself *these* questions, everything started to shift. There was no turning back. I had seen a therapist for 13 years who validated all the mistreatment I endured in relationships, but not once did we delve into why.

For years, I tried to make sense of the senseless situations that repeatedly played out in intimate relationships my entire adult life. I was angry, resentful, and completely unaware. I guess you could say that I'm a little late to the party, but I've been a late bloomer all my life.

I was late coming out of my mother's womb and late to hit my pubescent years. My older brothers teased me about it regularly. I didn't officially become a woman until I was nearly 14 years old, and I'm convinced that the muscles I used to hobble around on crutches after breaking my leg on an eighth grade ski trip were what finally prompted my buds to blossom. Thank God for small favors and for the faulty ski that didn't eject properly.

I suppose it should be no wonder that I find myself in my fifth decade still feeling a bit behind the eight ball when it comes to love, but I'm learning. My mother always said that her fifties were her best years. So here's to my fifth decade and the liberation that comes with midlife, where the need to discover and speak my truth is as necessary as the air that I breathe. A rite of passage comes with this age that allows us the freedom to talk more openly with far less fear of consequence.

This book is *not* simply about being midlife and single. It's about what I've learned during this stage that has absolutely changed my life. I spent decades in and out of abusive relationships—without even knowing it. For some people, that might be difficult to understand. How can anyone not know that they are being abused? Trust me, I asked myself the same question and was determined to figure out the answer —once and for all.

Looking back, I always knew that something wasn't right, but I couldn't put my finger on it, which is a trait that ties all targets of *narcissistic abuse* together: a gut feeling that something isn't right. Narcissistic abuse is composed of an endless array of insidious tactics that are used to manipulate, punish, and control. I never suffered a cut, bruise, nor broken bone, but the decline in my self-worth and self-esteem was immeasurable.

For me, a quick fix for the loneliness and misery I felt at the end of one dysfunctional relationship was to begin another. The adrenaline rush from each blossoming romance felt easy, carefree, and fun, like a coin tossed into a wide-open funnel with a momentum that allows it to effortlessly roll around and around. But, like the coin that eventually lowers into the narrowing cone, I repeatedly fell into spiraling vortexes of what I thought was love. We've all watched a coin whirling around in a coin funnel before being dropped into a black hole and trapped in the box below. Each time, I allowed "love" to trap me. But looking back now, I ask:

***Who*** was trapping me?

***Who*** was forcing me to stay?

***Why*** did the word "love" evoke in me such an immense feeling of duty to prove myself worthy no matter what?

When I didn't get the love that I desired and craved, I loved and gave more. In a game of tug-of-war, both sides begin with an equal amount of rope. In each relationship, the more I loved, the more slack I gave on the rope until it was all gone. When, in my last serious relationship, I found myself complaining like a broken record about the same things that I had complained about in previous relation-ships, a big, bright lightbulb went on! For the first time, I noticed something: The same relationship had been playing out throughout my life with different partners. While I had good reason to point my finger at every one of them for their bad behavior, I had never pointed back at myself. The common denominator in every one of my toxic relationships was *me!*

Wow, that was a revelation and a big, fat pill to swallow, like the blimp-shaped multi-vitamin I'm supposed to take every morning but conveniently forget because it never goes down easy. At the time, I had no idea what to do with my newfound awareness. I didn't know what it meant or what my next move was going to be, but I knew that it was going to lead me someplace different. It *had* to.

As I said before, this book is not really about being midlife and single. It's not about the abuse I endured nor my failed relationships. It's about something far more significant: AWARENESS. Once I had that, the rest began to fall into place.

I consider this book a detox, a cleanse, like vomiting up an *e coli*-infested burger that I downed hours ago. Be gone! Good riddance! It's about acknowledging the past to appreciate the present. What I have to say has all been said before, but I hope to say it a little differently. On the pages that follow, my wish is that what I openly share about my life will make a lightbulb come on for you. Then perhaps, the energy of your lightbulb will turn on another. And so on and so on.

We've all heard the saying, "You don't know where you are going until you know where you have been." It is very true, as long as the *awareness* of where you have been consists of acceptance and appreciation.

With that in mind, I begin this story at the end…

**Fact: Narcissistic abuse is an form of emotional and mental abuse perpetuated by people with Narcissistic Personality Disorder (NPD).**

## The End

"All great changes are preceded by chaos."—
Deepak Chopra

5 left, 38 right, 17 left. My hand shook as I wrote the numbers in permanent black marker on a note that I left for my kids on the kitchen table. I told them how much I loved them, gave a rather lengthy explanation of what I was about to do, and guided them to my hidden safe where they could find my last will and testament. Now, as I stand closer to the edge, I look out over the valley below. The cool, thin air rushes in through my nose with an ease I never experienced before.

I inch my feet toward the ledge with trepidation, knowing that the next step will be my last. My heart pounds faster, and the reality of what I am about to do drops like a two-ton brick upon my chest. I remind myself how I've wanted this for a long time and how well I've thought it through. I planned carefully, crossed all the Ts and dotted all the Is. It's the right decision that will be good for everyone. Backing out is not an option. I close my eyes, say a prayer, and fill my lungs one more time with the pristine air.

One final thought.

One final step.

And I fall.

"This is it," I think to myself, settling into the rushing air. "I actually did it."

Plummeting toward the earth feels nothing like I thought it would. Despite the speed at which I am falling, an unexpected stillness and a palpable clarity directly contrasts the fear and uncertainty of the moments before. Like every difficult decision I have ever made, I agonized over this for months, even years, delaying what I always knew in my heart would be the ultimate outcome. And for what? Countless migraines and antacids while I fretted over the unknown because I was too afraid to concede to the notion that sometimes, in some circumstances, the end is just the beginning.

**Fact: Narcissistic abuse can be difficult to identify because targets of the abuse don't feel comfortable coming forward with their experiences.**

# PART I
## Girl Gone Sad

# Clean Up in Aisle One

*When God wants you to grow, he makes you uncomfortable.*

Startled, I woke from the dream that had come to me before. The note, the jump, and the fall that seemed endless. I can't say that the reoccurring dream was a nightmare because I never hit the ground, and the fall always felt oddly soothing—in complete opposition to my conscious state.

It was Monday again, the beginning of a new week, and I had already hit the snooze button too many times for the morning to not be rushed. My husband hadn't come home after the argument we had the previous night. I had dared to question his whereabouts the day before when I drove past what looked like him and his young, female employee in *my* car. I saw them with my own two eyes as they raced past me with the top down in the convertible that he had surprised me with on my past birthday!

As many times as I had suspected him of cheating, I could never prove it. My suspicions were based mainly on a gut feeling that for 20 years, I had been groomed to doubt. But I clearly saw them: my husband with the young woman he had hired as his "assistant" in our business.

"You're fucking crazy!" he yelled. "Stop making shit up in your head. You're letting your insecurities get the best of you again."

After years of being told that I was paranoid and overly sensitive, part of me started to believe it to be true.

"I was nowhere near that road yesterday," he insisted, disgusted at being wrongly accused again. "Trust me, if I wanted to fuck her, I could, but I'm not, so don't worry about it. Seriously, if I was going to cheat, do you really think I would screw around with an employee rather than with someone out of town?" He chuckled as though his statement was supposed to reassure me. "Why are you always looking for problems? We would have a great marriage if you weren't so fucking insecure."

Once again, it was *my* fault.

"Ya know what," he said, switching his tone to the wrongly accused victim I had grown to expect. "Sometimes I think you *like* to argue. You must *want* our marriage to fail."

As usual, he stormed off. In the past, I would have called him to try to settle our disagreement. I would have been up all night wondering where he went. But over the years, I had somehow passed through that stage into a phase where his absence was somewhat of a relief, and sleep came easy, like a welcome escape from my reality.

The alarm sounded again. I had to get up, get the kids off to school, grocery shop, and pay some bills that had been piling up on my desk. But first, I lay still for one more minute to mentally prepare for the day. The moment of morning silence had become a daily ritual that I needed for my survival.

I stared up at the ceiling, tried to ignore the accumulation of dust on the ceiling fan, took a few deep breaths, and promised myself that I would keep it together for the sake of the kids. I had become good at faking it, but it seemed that the preparation for my daily act was growing far more taxing and far less effective. I would put a smile on my face and go about my routine. I had been doing it for years. I was a good wife and mother, active in the PTA, a soccer mom, and cheerleading coach. I worked out regularly and taught aerobics at our local community center. From the outside, it all looked good. I made sure of it.

That day was no different. At least it didn't seem so. I dropped the kids at school, stopped for coffee, and was on my way to the supermarket when it hit me again: the gnawing feeling that started in my stomach, crept up into my chest, and settled like a lump of sand in my throat. My heart raced, and the tingling began in my arms.

I felt for the pill bottle in my jacket pocket that the doctor prescribed for my "anxiety." Most of the time, it felt like an elephant sitting on my chest. The pressure had led me to the emergency room several times over the years, but the diagnosis was always the same: Anxiety. Pure and simple.

And the cure? Relax. Destress. Take deep breaths. Exercise. Do yoga. Try meditation. And if all else fails, pop a pill. The pill was the quickest and simplest way to relieve the stress of a situation I had not yet found the courage to confront. So I took them with me wherever I went, like a security blanket. Most of the time just having them was enough to get me through the day.

"*Fake it til you make it*" became my mantra. I became so good at faking it that most days, I was able to fool myself as much as the woman behind the deli counter who told me the same knock-knock joke almost every time I ordered a pound of cheese. I'd laugh, and find some small sense of pride in being able to fake it so well. But that day, the laugh didn't come. It was like the fake-laughter tank inside of me was suddenly, completely tapped out. Empty.

"Knock-knock."

"Who's there?" I asked.

"Tank."

"Tank who?"

"You're welcome," the lady at the deli said, handing me the white Cooper cheese that she had joyfully sliced. "Just the way you like it," she added, "And I stacked it so it won't stick together."

Something about her seemed genuinely happy, and I envied her for it. "Have a great day," she said and pressed the button for the next customer. "Number 36!" She turned to me before helping the man who approached the counter and gave me a lingering wink as though she knew I needed it.

I put the neatly sliced cheese into my cart and thought about how her life made her smile and mine made me cry. I ruminated over it as I scoured a produce bin for a few perfect lemons.

"She obviously doesn't have to deal with what I'm dealing with," I murmured, in a failed attempt to justify my misery. I began growing angry at a woman who I knew absolutely nothing about other than the fact that she was annoyingly blissful. How dare someone be so happy when I was so miserable! I grew angrier as I left the produce department and entered the frozen food section. Then something happened as I opened the freezer and reached for a box of buttermilk Eggos. Not the closest box, of course. I wanted a box in the back.

Being a smart, slightly germaphobic shopper, I reached further into the freezer to extract one that fewer people had handled. By the way, kudos to the Tetris pro who strategically stocked the freezer that day to best utilize every square inch of shelf space. It was a challenge I was not prepared for but one I was definitely not going to back away from, so I tugged and pulled, determined to get the box that I had my heart set on. I could have easily had another box, but I wanted *that* one. One way or another, it was coming with me.

I tugged, pulled, twisted, and turned until the cardboard box collapsed in my grip. With the irritation that percolated inside of me from the delightful Deli Diva, I gave the Eggos one final yank. It would have been a victory had the box not been supporting the shelf above it, which came crashing down in an avalanche of waffles and French toast sticks. I got a small cut on my hand, and there was a messy mound of frozen breakfast items piled up in the freezer, but I had my Eggos! I placed them in my cart and approached check-out.

Suddenly, as I looked down at the smashed box, it dawned on me how much time and energy I had wasted on something that didn't want to budge, instead of accepting its resistance, letting it go, and simply choosing another. In that moment, I hit a breaking point.

I had spent years in a terrible marriage, doing the same thing and hoping for a different result. As I left the supermarket, I dropped the crumpled box of Eggos into the garbage and decided to do something completely out of character. Defense had obviously not been working for me, so I switched to the big "O." For the first time ever, I began to take back control of *my* life.

**Fact: The narcissistic abuse cycle is a pattern of behavior that typically consists of four phases: idealization, devaluation, discarding, and hoovering.**

## Fake It til You Make It—Or Not

*Never allow your current situation to be your final destination.*

No one ever knew how bad my marriage was. In all honesty, I didn't know either. Over the years, it had crept up on me, like ivy on the side of a building.

I justified my husband's inexcusable behavior and questioned whether or not it was me being exactly what he always claimed I was: oversensitive, insecure, paranoid, and weak. His threats of infidelity, verbal assaults, and lies had become a regular part of the day, something that I had adjusted to.

I argued back, laughed it off, or ignored it all together with the hope that one day something I would say or do would make him stop, but the more I tolerated, the worse he became. I felt like a puppet on the hand of a ventriloquist, manipulated and controlled by a master puppeteer.

My moods became merely a reflection of his, and any joy I experienced was based solely on what he would allow me to have. In the name of love, I relinquished ALL my control. Manipulation is a powerful tool when the one being manipulated is unaware. Sadly, I didn't realize that I was being abused until I had built my life around him. Precious years had passed, and yet I was stuck in the same spot where I began, living in a constant state of hypervigilance where I walked on eggshells around a man who declared his love for me every day.

Something had to change, and for the first time, I knew that something had to be me. My mental, emotional, and physical health were on the line, and I had to take action. It was clearly the only way to change course.

If one's mind set is right, being a detective doesn't require any training. All that is needed is a hunch, backed by emotion, and fueled by the insanity that comes when you're told that you're being ridiculous, overthinking, or making shit up in your head. There's no shortage of cleverness when you have had enough.

I waited until my husband was out of town for the day so I would have plenty of time to search his office. I opened every drawer, searched each file cabinet, and rummaged through the trash cans. If you wait long enough, even the most conniving and sneaky person gets sloppy. Or maybe he wasn't sloppy at all. Maybe he had become so damned arrogant and entitled that he didn't give a shit if I found women's names and numbers on the back of business cards, receipts for flowers and hotel rooms, and love letters shoved deep into a desk drawer written to the man who I shared a

bed with every night—the same man who stood before me
and vowed to love and cherish me, 'til death do us part.

When I reached into a suitcoat pocket and pulled out a
picture of his assistant sitting on his lap, I felt victorious.
When I pulled out a pair of her used underwear, I felt sick.

*I knew it!*

As it turned out, every suspicion I had was true. Every
instinct was spot on, and then some. Lies, lies, lies. I walked
through every room of the office that I had furnished and
organized for our "family business." I fantasized about the
damage I could do as I imagined slamming his leather chair
into the flat-screen tv and shredding the cushions of the full-
size sofa he had to have in case he ever had to spend the
night in an office that was only 20 minutes from home. I
wanted everything to be completely unsalvageable.

And then I did what anyone would do in that very moment
when faced with an undeniable, life-altering betrayal. Not
really. I actually did what anyone who had been horribly
brainwashed and threatened for years would do. I gulped
down the rage that boiled up inside of me as the fear that
had been so ingrained in me took over:

*What if his threats are real?*

*What if he harms me?*

*What if he takes the kids?*

*What if he leaves me with nothing?*

*What if?*

*What if?*

*What if?*

With the photo in hand and my heart pounding in my chest, I grabbed a large jar of coins on his desk, drew my arm back into position, and turned toward the television. I had never been angry like that before. It felt as though the person I am had been hijacked by a crazy, out-of-control impersonator. I never yelled and screamed at anyone—until I met him. I was never jealous and insecure—until I met him. And I was never someone who wanted to hurl something across the room—until that very moment.

Luckily, somewhere inside of me was the *real* me, the girl I had lost along the way. Her voice of reason begged to be heard. Losing control would give him reason to tell others "she's crazy."

Losing control would allow him to win, so I lowered my arm, tipped over the coin jar, and watched the coins scatter across his desk, spill onto the floor, and roll beneath the bookshelf where I had placed framed photos of our children. I grabbed the frames, went back to my car, and stared at the picture of his infidelity before noticing my daughter's favorite tote bag on the passenger's seat from a recent sleep-over. The bag was filled with the items of a young teen—*our* young teen: pajamas, a toothbrush, lip gloss. I looked again at the picture, then the tote, sickened at how I allowed something so sinful to get close to something so innocent.

My jaw tightened. I grabbed the tote, dumped everything out of it, and held it to my mouth, filling it with the apple muffin I ate for breakfast along with the gut feeling that had been churning in my stomach for years. I disposed of the tote in a Dumpster behind Walmart and returned home where I waited to confront him with the evidence.

I listened to endless excuses and justifications. I witnessed tears of sorrow as he begged me to stay and promised to change. Like the ebb and flow of the ocean, my anger receded just enough to allow his charming maleficence to seep in again. So I did what any good wife, good mother, and completely oblivious *codependent* would do who desperately wanted to believe in the man she had built her life around. I ran to the mall to buy my daughter another tote, and I gave that son-of-a-bitch one more chance.

**Fact: Long-term narcissistic abuse can change a victim's brain, resulting in cognitive decline and memory loss.**

# The Big Spill

_The one who angers you, controls you._

"Hey, it's me," Mare said when she called. "How ya doin?"

Mare was a neighbor in the development where we had recently built our new home. When we first met, we had connected instantly. I'm a Jersey girl, and Mare's from South Philly with the accent to prove it. She was the only person I knew who, like me, put on a pair of big hoop earrings in the morning before getting dressed and didn't take them off until climbing into bed at night.

One morning after a long walk, I spilled my guts to her. Truth is, I would have spilled my guts to anyone that day. She just happened to be the first lucky girl to cross my path as she walked out to get the paper with a cup of coffee in one hand and Roxie, her teacup Yorkie, in the other.

"Hey, Shar, how's it goin'?" Mare asked as she put Roxie down on the patch of grass she had designated for doggie doo-doo.

I lowered my baseball cap so she wouldn't see how blood-shot my eyes were from my early morning meltdown.

"Good," I lied as I walked closer. "How have you been?"

Mare picked up the paper, made a comment about the headline, and took a sip from her mug before noticing Roxie in an area of recently treated lush green lawn.

"Don't you dare!" she yelled as Roxie assumed the position by her newly mulched flower bed. Mare shook her head in disgust. "Jesus Christ," she said, "Remind me again why I said yes to the kids getting a dog, knowing damn well that I would be the only one taking care of her?"

I shrugged my shoulders and managed a sympathetic expression.

Mare took another sip of coffee and checked to make sure the Velcro hair roller in the crown of her head was still intact. "I swear that goddamn dog wants to destroy every-thing I have. Look at her," she said, locking eyes with the five-pound ball of fur who strained to finish. "It's like she's doing it on purpose."

Mare was pretty funny, and I often wished I had her prob-lems instead of mine. "Do you know how much money we just spent on landscaping? The cost of lawncare these days is ridiculous."

"I hear ya," I said, staring up into the early morning sky. In a moment of awkward silence that followed, I thought about trying to convince her that it was the sun causing my eyes to tear. But no thought could override the fact that every cell in my body had reached its limit. "My marriage is over," I said and looked away so I wouldn't see her expression. For years, the thick, tight feeling in the back of my throat had been like a well-constructed dam that had successfully suppressed a tidal wave of emotions. And in that very moment, it broke wide open—all over Mare.

"What?" The shock on her face mirrored the shock I felt in saying it. "What are you talking about? What happened?"

"For starters, he cheated on me," I said, forcing my ego to step aside. Saying those four words hurt. But holding them in hurt even more.

"Are you serious?" she asked, positioning herself directly in front of me. She leaned in and looked me in the eye to determine whether or not I was bullshitting. "Are you sure?"

"Yes, I'm sure," I answered without hesitating. "He cheated on me, and I'm sure it's not the first time, and I don't think she's the first one. I think there have been many."

Mare wrapped her arm around me and led me into her kitchen.

"The signs have been there for a long time," I said. "I guess I didn't want to face it."

Mare placed a coffee mug in front of me and filled it to the rim. "How did you find out?" she asked.

"I was in the frozen food section last week, when something hit me," I said.

"Oh my God, you were hit by something in the grocery store?" She pulled the roller out of her hair.

"Yeah…I mean no…something actually did hit me, but that's a different story." I lifted the mug to my mouth, "What I mean is that something changed that day. It's hard to explain, but it was like I couldn't lie to myself anymore about my marriage."

Mare pulled up a chair beside me and sat down on the edge, intently fixed on my story.

"My marriage has never been good," I said, shaking my head. "Never."

She put her hand on mine. "He treats me like shit, and for some reason, I keep putting up with it. I don't know if he's ever told me the truth about anything. I've always had a feeling that something was going on behind my back, but I could never prove it, so after all these years, I finally found the courage to go looking for it," I said, hating that my life had become like a soap opera. Drama, drama, drama. "And you know what?" I asked, looking out the window at our beautiful new house a few doors down. "I fucking found it."

———

Mare was the first person I opened up to, and since that morning she calls me every day.

"How ya doin'?"

"Well, I'm not hanging from the chandelier yet," I joked. "So I guess it's a good day."

"Oh thank God," she said, "because the chandelier in your house is way too high. I'd need stripper pumps to reach you, and I haven't owned a pair of those in years."

"Who am I kidding," I confessed. "With all the muffins I've been eating lately, that chandelier wouldn't even hold me. I'd come crashing down and end up with a broken ankle at best."

She laughed, and I found a bit of relief in the meaningless banter. "Seriously, I'm hanging in there, no pun intended."

"Well, at least you're keeping your sense of humor," she said. "It's important. Ya know what I'm sayin'?

"Yes, I know what you're sayin'." Mare was good at lightening the load for a few minutes, but as soon as we hung up, reality set in. If the universe was trying to point me somewhere, I was in trouble because I have absolutely no sense of direction. When God was handing out directional capabilities, I was definitely in the handbag section. The truth was although I had given in to his tears and empty apologies, I had come to a two-pronged fork in the road, and there was no turning back. One road was the one I'd been on for years, filled with potholes, muddy puddles, and heaping piles of shit that I tiptoed around in a continuous dance of avoidance. The other road, although unclear and untraveled, offered something new that I hadn't felt in years: a teeny-tiny ray of optimism.

**Fact: On average, victims of narcissistic abuse will return to their abuser seven or eight times before leaving for good.**

# The Turban and the Squirrel

Enough is a decision, not an amount.

"We don't kiss anymore," I said, throwing off the covers after reluctantly agreeing to some "afternoon delight." "As a matter of fact, we haven't kissed in years." I got out of bed and threw my robe on while my husband casually walked to the other side of the room butt-naked.

After 20 years, our bodies were not what they used to be, and I remember marveling at how he could be so confident in the light of day. A few months had passed since I caught him cheating. For me, every minute of every day was a challenge, and it pissed me off that he walked around seemingly unaffected. It was like he shit all over me and didn't even have the courtesy to wipe it off. He picked up his phone and graced me with a glance.

"What are you talking about?" he asked. Once again, his phone captured his undivided attention as he took a seat on the edge of the bed and scrolled through an endless list of texts.

"I'm talking about *us* and how we haven't kissed or even touched each other with any affection in years," I said. I picked up a basket of laundry, set it down on the bed, and began picking through a crumpled load of whites that I left in the dryer for way too long. I pulled out a towel and tripped on his shoes as I walked toward the bathroom to rinse him off me because I felt dirty and used again.

"Do you know how many times I've asked you *not* to leave your shoes in the middle of the floor?" I said, kicking them to the side.

His phone beeped to alert him of a new text, and he laughed a little while typing back an answer before responding.

"What?" he asked with his head still in his phone.

"You're not even listening to me."

"What is your fucking problem?" he yelled.

"This," I said, pointing back and forth between the two of us, "is my problem. All of this. Forget about how we don't *kiss* or touch anymore; we don't even talk! Your mind is always somewhere else, and mine is always here, on you and the kids and on trying to figure out a way to make this work. But I can't do it alone, and that's exactly how I feel, completely alone!"

"Here we go again," he said, pulling up the black dress socks that he hadn't bothered taking off. "And you wonder why I'm never home. I can't fucking deal with this."

"You told me you *wanted* this," I said, turning on the shower. "You said you wanted to make this work, *remember*? What about the tears and the apologies? You're not even trying! And who are you texting? Who is it this time?" I made the water as hot as I could stand and washed away yet another afternoon mistake.

"I'm so sick of hearing the same shit!" he yelled from the other side of the shower door. "You're like a broken record. If you're not happy, then do something about it!" The sound of his pants zipper sliced through the noise of the pulsating water that rained down over my head. I turned off the water, reached for a towel, and stepped out of the shower.

"And what about that smell in the bedroom that I've been telling you about," I said, changing the subject to another household matter that he chose to dismiss. I dried myself off and wrapped my hair in a well-configured towel turban while he stood in front of the mirror adjusting his tie. "Something reeks in there," I said, pointing into the master bedroom that adjoined the bathroom of our newly constructed home. "Don't you smell it?" I asked, shimmying my damp skin into a T-shirt and pair of jeans that had become too tight.

I bent my knees to stretch the denim while assuring myself that it was that damn new dryer shrinking my clothes rather than admitting to the bagel shop runs that had become a morning ritual after dropping the kids off at school. Over the past few months, I had managed to convince myself that the apples in the apple crumb muffin made it a healthy breakfast choice and that I needed it to combat the stress that I was dealing with. I walked into the bedroom, lifted my nose into the air, and sniffed. "It smells like a dead animal!" I said, tugging my jeans up over the appropriately named "muffin top" that had never been there before. I tried to trace the foul stench that had been bothering me for weeks.

"Yeah right, it's a dead animal," he said, dismissing me with an irritation I had grown used to. I sniffed again, following the odor. "Look at you," he said, with a smug grin that I despised. "You look like a fucking idiot."

The pounds he had put on over the years were far more noticeable than mine, and I laughed to myself at the way his love handles protruded over his pants. He squeezed into his suitcoat and doused himself with too much cologne as he often did. The battle inside my mind raged on. The way he treated me was wrong. Very wrong. Wasn't it? Surely other people would agree. The mind games he played on a daily basis had me spinning and doubting everything about myself, my thoughts, and my feelings.

"I can't believe you don't smell it!" I said, walking around the room. I dropped to the floor, looked under the bed, and with my turban still intact, crawled around the perimeter of our bedroom where the odor seemed to strengthen.

"You don't know what you're talking about," he sneered. "It's coming from outside. We *are* in the middle of the woods, remember *Einstein*?"

After years of being insulted and disrespected, I was more determined than ever to prove him wrong, so I continued on, narrowing in on the outer wall that faced the back woods.

"I bet something got into the attic or one of the walls and couldn't get out," I muttered to assure myself. "It's here somewhere. I know it."

"You're wasting your time," he said and grabbed his keys to leave.

"Yeah well, my instincts have been spot on before, haven't they?" I said, making a comment I knew would reignite a war. I looked back at the man who, over the years, had become my archenemy.

"How long do I have to pay for it anyway?" he asked and slammed his fist into the wall. "I cheated on you, big fucking deal! Get over it!" His disregard of my feelings normally pushed me to fury or tears, but that day I felt nothing. For the first time in nearly 20 years, as I stared at another hole in the wall, I actually felt nothing.

"Get over it," I said, repeating his words as though hearing them for the first time. "Get over it," I murmured again and again like a guiding affirmation as I continued to inspect every crevasse of the back wall. "Get over it, get over it, get over it."

My mother told me that one day I would have enough and that when that day came, I would just know it. "Every worm turns," she said with an assurance well-rooted in wisdom. And she was right. In that very moment, I got over it. Like flipping off a light switch, I was done. I got up off the floor, yanked my jeans up over my bagel shop bulge, dumped the remaining clothes from the laundry basket onto the bed, and walked to his closet. "I gave you 20 years," I said, filling the basket with his clothes. "The next 20 are mine."

I went to the kitchen, grabbed a box of garbage bags from under the sink, and returned to the closet. As he watched in disbelief, I cleared every shelf. I pulled every garment off its hanger and stuffed them into the scented bags that I had recently bought to fill the beautiful new trash bins in the beautiful new kitchen of our beautiful new home. Everything around me was beautiful and new, but what filled the beautiful new rooms was an ugly, old mess—a 20-year-old mess, to be exact, accumulated by 20 years of sweeping the mess under the carpet and walking around with blinders on. While I scrambled to finish the job, he mumbled something foul under his breath as he always did to intimidate. It didn't take me long to empty his entire closet, carry the bags to the front door, and heave every last one of them out onto the porch. He didn't try to stop me. On some level, he must have known that he couldn't. Or maybe he was mildly intimidated by a woman in a turban and uncomfortably tight jeans.

"Get out!" I said, standing by the open door.

He clenched his teeth, and I watched as his jawbone rippled beneath his skin. "You'll fucking regret this," he threatened.

"Wait!" I said as he picked up a few bags and stepped off the front porch step. "You forgot something!" I pulled the diamond ring off my left finger, the one he bought to replace the old one because he was "thinking of me" on his last, so-called, business trip. I threw it at him as hard as I could, slammed the door, leaned against it, and waited for the sound of his car to pull away before taking a breath.

I stared at the white indentation on my ring finger, left behind from 20 years of wear, 20 years of broken promises, 20 years of tears. I wondered why I waited so long to leave someone who made me so sad, and I promised myself that I would never, ever let him in again. "Hell hath no fury like a woman scorned" might be true, but even truer is "hell hath no fury like a woman who is told that she is making shit up in her head!" So I ran to the garage, grabbed a hammer, and returned to the bedroom where I paused for a moment while contemplating whether or not I should do it.

"What if I'm wrong?" I asked out loud, allowing the doubt that he poured into me for 20 years to surface again. All the names I had been called throughout our marriage played in my head like a broken record. I was a "fucking idiot," a "worthless cunt," and a "weak bitch" to name a few, but the list goes on.

To this day, I struggle with how I lived in such chaos for so long. I don't believe anyone truly understands how insidious abuse can be unless they've experienced it. It doesn't happen overnight, and it certainly doesn't happen all the time. A master manipulator can be the sweetest, kindest, most generous person one minute and the devil the next. I stared at the picture that I used to cover the last hole that his fist went through when I first accused him of cheating. It read "Live, Laugh, Love." There had never been any of that in our bedroom, so with all the strength I could muster, I slammed the hammer into the wall, tearing open the drywall to the hollow cavity beneath it.

When I accused him of being unfaithful, he called me ridiculous and insecure. I felt powerless because I felt his lies right through to my bones. Every instinct in my body told me he was cheating. I knew it, but I could never prove it. So I recklessly drove the hammer into the wall again, choking on the drywall dust that rained down on me until a maggot-infested squirrel fell from the wall and plopped onto the floor by my feet. I didn't gasp nor shriek nor jump because I knew it. I just had to prove it. Looking down at the decaying carcass, I dropped the hammer and despite the pungent odor, inhaled the deepest, most satisfying breath I had taken in two decades. I lifted the "Live, Laugh, Love" picture from the wall to expose the ugly truth that I had shamefully concealed for nearly 20 years. I flipped open my cell and pressed the number 1 that I had devotedly designated to my husband.

"What?" he asked when he answered. The irritation in his voice was the final nail in the coffin.

"It's me," I said in a calm, steady voice that I had never found in my marriage. "I want a divorce." I hung up the phone, pulled the dusty turban off my head, and unbuttoned my jeans because, like him, they no longer fit.

**Fact: Often, narcissists won't let you go, even when they're with a new partner.**

# PART II

# Girl Gone Mad

## Nothing Changes if Nothing Changes

*Awareness is the greatest agent for change.*

Realizing I was in an abusive marriage was difficult, but what was even more difficult was admitting to myself that telling him I wanted a divorce that day was like playing my best hand in a game of cards. A part of me still thought that a separation would be so impactful that he would actually change! Unbelievable!

That is a true testament to how brainwashed I was into thinking I deserved nothing more. For years, I allowed myself to be controlled and manipulated. It was a vicious cycle of repeatedly being chewed up, spit out, and sucked back in. I tried everything I could think of to change someone whose agenda was simply **not** to change—as I would come to learn.

I continually set boundaries and enforced none. The abuse I endured often made me feel like I was losing my mind. His weapons of choice were name-calling and mind games. The most horrific, vile words rolled off his tongue with ease one minute, and the next he was professing his undying love for me or gaslighting me by denying what he had said all together.

"Everyone argues and says things they don't mean," he would laugh. "Big deal. I say stupid shit sometimes, but I love you. That's what really matters. Stop making such a big deal out of nothing."

What he said was true: Everyone *does* argue, and people *can* say things in anger that they don't mean, so maybe I *was* making a big deal out of nothing, but I was dying inside, hemorrhaging from somewhere deep within. For the life of me, I couldn't figure out how to make it stop.

Kicking him out only gave him an excuse for doing more of the same. He played the victim to friends and family as well as the female prospects whose support and sympathy he had gained over the years by creating a **smear campaign** about his miserable wife who was never happy nor satisfied with anything. Still, I was not ready to admit absolute defeat and give up on our family nor the time and energy that I had invested over the years.

Like trying to pick up a bead of liquid mercury, the answer seemed so simple and yet so impossible. In the months that followed, I tried everything to get him to understand that the way he was treating me was the cause of our problems. The person he made me out to be only made me try harder to change our situation because who wants to be known as miserable, unhappy, and unsatisfied? I wasn't who he claimed I was. Was I? Throughout our separation, the cycle continued. I was met with disdain and denial on one day and loving promises of a bright future another. The only predictability to his moods was to show no remorse, no regret, no accountability, and no empathy.

"The only thing I care about is sex and money," he admitted one day when he dropped by to pick up a few things.

I froze with the shock and awe of such a statement. I remember stuttering a bit with confusion and disbelief. "W...what? Why would you say that?"

He looked me in the eyes and shrugged his shoulders. Upstairs, our son and daughter were in their bedrooms doing teenage things like listening to music, playing video games, and talking on the phone.

I wanted to yell and scream and pound on his chest. "That can't be true! Tell me that isn't true! You don't mean that!" But more than anything, in that moment, I wanted to hurt him.

After 20 years of him calling me a "worthless bitch" one minute and telling me how much he loved me the next, my mind was scrambled. I was being mind-fucked daily. The result was more self-doubt as I questioned everything I thought I knew and more **self-abandonment** as I completely deserted my own wants and needs for his.

The truth is, nothing he ever did *felt* like love, yet that word kept me imprisoned in a life of misery for years. Why would someone who "loves" me treat me this way? If he "loves" me, he'll change, and we can make this work. He must not understand what I want and need from him. Maybe if I try harder and love him more, he'll "get it" and change.

During our separation, my life became a dizzying, endless ride on a carousel of abuse. Round and round and round. I gave; he took. I bent; he remained rigid. On his part, there was no flexibility and certainly no compromise—unless it was in his best interest. He stayed at a hotel but occasionally stopped by to stir the pot. Some days he would sweep in with a smile on his face to tell me how much he loved and missed me.

"You know I say stupid things sometimes. It doesn't mean I don't love you. We can make this work. I know we can. I love you to death." As he had done throughout our marriage, he gave me just enough to keep me hanging on to the hope that he was going to change. He promised to go back to church and seek counseling.

Once again, I held on to the possibility that with the help of professionals, we could reconcile for the sake of our family. But when the weeks and months that followed yielded nothing more than the same behavior, filing for divorce seemed more unavoidable than ever.

I was scared, plain and simple, but despite my fear, I began to push back. Taking steps to begin divorce proceedings made the abuse ramp up even more. Nothing pisses off an abuser more than realizing that their victim is slipping from their grip. His lies, insults, and threats became more frequent as did the teary-eyed promises. It was a roller-coaster of mood swings like never before. He was a desperate man acting like a toddler who couldn't get his way.

His range of threats vacillated between reminding me of how many other women he could "fuck," to threats of taking his life or mine if I didn't take him back. When I told him that I was going to see an attorney to file for divorce, he laughed. "With what?" he asked, "You need money, dumb-ass, and you don't have shit without me. Besides, what do you think some dip-shit local attorney is gonna do for you? I can hire the best attorneys in the country, who will eat your attorney for breakfast and destroy you, so don't be so fucking stupid. You'll be left on the street with nothing."

He stood close, puffed out his chest, and bumped into me hard enough to knock me off balance. When I stumbled back, he grabbed onto me so I wouldn't fall. "You're so weak," he laughed, proud of the physical strength he displayed against someone 90 pounds less. "Do you know what I could do to you?" He leaned in closer. "You have no idea who I am or what I'm capable of."

He held his teeth together and spoke in a low tone that rested somewhere between a joke and a promise. "Don't make me show you." He grinned and laughed before releasing his grip from my arms. He looked down at his phone to read through some messages. "I'm hungry. You got anything to eat?"

Over the years, his threats had gradually grown bolder and far more graphic. I had become desensitized. His venomous words didn't mean as much, and they certainly didn't have the same sting after years of them. A part of me wanted to call him out on every single threat by telling him what a coward I thought he was. I wanted to dare him to actually act on something for once rather than simply bullying me into submission. At this point, you're probably wondering:

*Why did I stay?*

I had a lot of work to do to figure out the answer to that question. Had I not lived it, I would have a very difficult time understanding why anyone would stay in such an abusive relationship. Over the years, I had adapted to his drastic mood swings. Every low was followed by a high, every explosive argument was followed by a tender makeup, and every threat was followed by a justification. I found a distorted sense of comfort in knowing that after such a sinister "down," there was a thrilling "up" around the corner. So I held out every time.

The physical, mental, and emotional exhaustion that I endured made any other option seem far too daunting. My expectations had been managed down so low that I felt a sense of joy on days when he behaved well or would simply ignore me rather than attack me. Back then, I never considered that words and threats without bumps and bruises were abuse, but I finally became depressed enough to realize that I needed help.

I didn't know what that meant or where I was going to get it, but I began talking more openly to anyone I could trust. Although I had confided in Mare about the infidelity and mistreatment, I had never spoken with her in detail about the mental and verbal abuse. For the first time, I opened up about what I had been going through, from the erratic mood swings to the lies and threats.

"It sounds like he has a personality disorder," she said, as we browsed through cookbooks at Barnes & Noble.

"A what?" I asked, feeling a little embarrassed of my lack of knowledge on the topic.

"A personality disorder," she said, leading me to the mental health section where, for the first time in 20 years, I found what seemed like an explanation for the madness. All signs pointed to **narcissism.** It all made sense, and I felt somewhat relieved to have found the problem that had plagued our relationship for so many years. Knowing the problem is the first step to fixing it, right?

Those were the days before Google and YouTube, so I bought books to help me understand. As always, I devoted most of my time and attention to figuring him out. I didn't know where that would lead, but I felt encouraged that with a proper diagnosis and professional help, maybe, just maybe, he could change!

Sadly, at the time, I thought that was enough.

**Fact: Narcissists see people as resources to be used for their own gain.**

## The Hazards of Hope

*Nothing in life stops until it has taught us what we needed to learn.*

*He is disrespectful, but I'll respect him and **hope** that he will change.*

*He ignores me, but I'll give him all my attention and **hope** that he will change.*

*He makes me sad, but I'll try to make him happy and **hope** that he will change.*

*He puts me last, but I'll put him first and **hope** that he will change.*

*He puts little effort into the relationship, but I'll try harder and **hope** that he will change.*

*He betrays me, but I'll be loyal to him and **hope** that he will change.*

*He criticizes me, but I'll give him compliments and **hope** that he will change.*

*He puts me down, but I'll lift him up and **hope** that he will change.*

*He has secrets, but I'll share everything and* **hope** *that he will change.*

*He doesn't make me feel loved, but I'll make him feel loved and* **hope** *that he will change.*

For people who have never experienced a long-term relationship with a narcissist, the above statements sound absurd. Commonsense tells us that only a fool would give so much to someone who returns so little. But, regardless of the abuse, victims often endure years of misery yet still feel unable to leave the relationship. The unhealthy attachment to their abuser, known as a **trauma bond**, is made up of highs and lows, rewards and punishments.

Targets of narcissistic abuse are unknowingly conditioned to anticipate the high after every low and the reward after every punishment. These learned expectations can keep them holding on to hope that the highs and rewards will prevail.

In most circumstances, hope is positive. It represents optimism for a desired outcome. But in a relationship with a narcissist, hope can be the very thing that keeps us tied to a runaway train that is headed off the tracks. Narcissists keep their victims hooked on hope by using intermittent reinforcements and **future faking**, making promises they *never* intend to keep. I held on to hope for decades.

When the verbal abuse first began several months into our relationship, he convinced me that his words didn't matter. "I'm kidding. It was a joke. I say stupid things sometimes," he'd say. "I love you. I didn't mean it. You know that. I'm really stressed out right now, that's all. Things will be better when we live together."

I trusted and believed in him so that's what we did, but the verbal attacks continued, as well as the insults disguised as jokes that often pushed me to tears. Each time he broke me down, he lifted me back up with reassurances. "I'm sorry. Don't cry. I love you to death. You know that," he'd say. "I was joking around with you. You're so sensitive. Your family must have sheltered you your whole life. All we need is some space. Once we get married and move away from here everything will be better. I promise."

I became completely emotionally and mentally **enmeshed** in a relationship that was based solely on what he promised it would be—rather than what it actually was. In the process, I lost sight of my own wants and needs. Part of me became controlled by the fear of the monster he would occasionally become and another part of me held on to a future that I was assured of. Drunk on hope, I agreed to marry him. Throughout our marriage, he told me he loved me several times a day, which despite his abuse and threats made me believe that he actually did and that he would never harm me. But the truth is that he *was* harming me every day with his lies, betrayals, insults, and mind games. And when *he* wasn't lying to me, *I* was lying to myself!

**Cognitive dissonance** is like a war that happens within our "self." Our inner being, detecting harm, fights to protect us from what our heart is desiring, while our brain is caught somewhere in the middle, registering the mistreatment and yet justifying it at the same time. It is a constant internal battle that causes physical, emotional, and mental distress. Let me be very clear, abusers are *not* abusive all the time. There are good times throughout the relationship, especially in the beginning, otherwise known as the **love-bombing**

phase, which can easily be confused with the honeymoon phase of a relationship.

Every romantic relationship has one, but the difference lies in the intention. Narcissists can be extremely affectionate, attentive, funny, charming, compassionate, and nurturing. They can shower us in attention, compliments, sex, gifts, and trips, or they can make us feel sorry for them by telling us sad stories of their past and/or current situation. They can woo, seduce, or play the victim to secure their target. They can pretend to be everything we ever wanted by carefully crafting a false image to win us over and keep us in a relationship that *they need* to satisfy their own wants and needs. They will tell us we are the love of their life, their fate, their destiny, the only one they've ever truly loved. They can make us feel like the luckiest person in the world to have finally met "the one." A narcissist will place us high on a pedestal where we feel on top of the world.

But the problem is that there's only room for one foot on that pedestal, and we're balancing up there in the middle of a hurricane! So when we inevitably fall off, and we all do, by questioning their bad behavior, attempting to hold them accountable, or defending ourselves, we become faulty in their eyes and no longer deserving of their supposed true love and affection. In essence, when we begin to stand up for ourselves, we are seen as imperfect for daring to ask for the love and respect that we deserve. A narcissist will expect to be loved, served, complimented, worshiped, and adored from the people whom they criticize, minimize, belittle, insult, betray, and demean. They feel entitled to the devout loyalty of others while offering nothing more than lies and deception.

For decades, I balanced on a pedestal in the wind. I was repeatedly punished for falling off and rewarded by being placed back onto a smaller one. As the years passed, regardless of how hard I tried, I was more off than on. I told myself everything would be okay because I was too afraid to admit the truth. The truth is that I was teetering on the edge of sanity, day in and day out, trying desperately to satisfy someone who would *never* be satisfied. I could never *do* enough, *be* enough, *give* enough, or *love* enough to someone who could *never get* enough.

Narcissists are empty, bottomless vessels, insatiable to their core. They selfishly take from others and only give back when it is in their best interest. Throughout the relationship, they will intermittently present a charming, false self to show us how good the relationship *can* be, and then they pull that away to keep us hungering for the behavior that we love. That hunger keeps us hooked. While the narcissist is addicted to attention, the partner becomes addicted to hope.

Throughout my marriage, I danced around the abuse by justifying his poor behavior. Too many times, I took the bait and blamed myself for being overly sensitive, unable to take a joke, insecure, and paranoid as he always accused me of on occasions when I called him out on my suspicions. The **intermittent reinforcements** kept me balancing on a shaky fence between realities. On one side was what he wanted me to continue to believe: that all our problems were in my head and our marriage would be great if I would just stop "overthinking" everything. He needed to keep me in that frame of mind so that he could continue to have full control.

On the other side was a glimmer of truth. And in that glimmer, albeit very small, there was a budding desire for something different, something better. The battle in my head was exhausting. The undeserving trust that I willingly gave yielded me nothing more than complete financial dependency on him. Every time I thought of a reason to leave, I thought of another not to. Every time I thought about how I could make it on my own, I feared that I couldn't.

The most troubling part of it all was how invisible I had become. It was like he had erased a small part of me each and every day until there was no trace of the person I once was and no room for the person I was meant to be.

Eventually, as my physical and mental health began to deteriorate from the unrelenting stress, I leaned into the glimmer of truth and the dream of saving myself. The decision to once and for all file for divorce was like being led to a cliff by a pride of hungry lions at my back, with two possible outcomes: one sure demise and the other to step off the cliff and be caught by a net that I prayed was somewhere down there to catch me.

It took nearly 20 years of abuse to admit the ugly truth and become desperate enough to summon up the courage to stop the cycle. I learned a lot from that relationship, but not nearly enough. Ending it might have calmed the waters, but what muddied them had yet to surface. Ending my marriage was like opening my eyes ever so slightly after having them shut for years. The light was blinding after being in the dark for so long.

My husband's abuse and infidelity are *not* what ended our marriage. We never really had one. A signed piece of paper and a few words before a minister does not guarantee respect, loyalty, and devotion. Our relationship, built on deception and false promises, was doomed from the beginning. Unfortunately, I was the last one to know it.

Narcissists are among us, in all genders, races, and classes. The disorder does not discriminate. They are toxic beings, capable of destroying lives without a care or second thought, and the love they profess is based solely on what they can extract from their source. Survivors describe them as being evil, empty souls who treat people as objects that are to be used for their benefit or pleasure and discarded when the thrill is gone or they are no longer needed.

It sounds unthinkable and it is, but a narcissist is both appealing and cunning, which is how they manage to get by on the stage of life. They are great actors, wolves in sheep's clothing, masters of deception, believing that they are entitled to and deserving of nothing less than the best. They do the most damage to the people they pretend to love. Like a cancer, they slowly eat away at the heart and soul of their victims by building them up and tearing them down, over and over again. It is a sadistic cycle.

Someone with narcissistic personality disorder (NPD) can be difficult to clinically diagnose because narcissists rarely seek professional help for failed relationships or personal problems that they believe are everyone else's fault. Their lack of self-awareness and self-reflection, as well as their inability to take accountability for their actions and bad behavior, prevent them from forming healthy connections. They are addicted to both positive and negative attention, thrive on the drama and chaos that they go out of their way to create, and have an overinflated sense of superiority that masks their fragile egos and extreme insecurities.

In time, a target of narcissistic abuse loses their self-worth, suffers from physical ailments, and questions their own sanity. The effects can be detrimental, which is why it is so important to be aware of the red flags of narcissism and the symptoms of narcissistic abuse.

**Fact: One of the patterns in a relationship with a narcissist involves frequent breakups and makeups.**

## The Red Flags of Narcissism

*Inner peace begins the moment you choose not to allow another person or event to control your emotions.*

It is important to note that narcissism exists on a spectrum and that we all possess *some* narcissistic traits. Individuals who are high on the spectrum, in other words, exhibit many of the traits listed below, are considered to have NPD, Narcissistic Personality Disorder. These individuals are rarely diagnosed by a professional because they seldom seek help for relationship problems that they believe are someone else's fault. Narcissists are master manipulators who lack self-awareness and self-reflection. If they are coerced into therapy via an ultimatum, you can expect an Academy Award-winning performance that rarely results in long lasting growth or improvement.

- Self-centered
- Arrogant and overly confident

- Feels superior to others
- Entitled
- Brags
- Needs admiration
- Controlling and manipulative
- Puts their needs first
- Uses flattery, belittling, or threats to get what they want
- Lacks empathy
- Passive-aggressive
- Spiteful
- Secretive
- Inconsistent
- Seeks revenge when they feel wronged in any way
- Highly sensitivity to criticism
- Extremely critical of you and others
- Teases and mocks
- Disguises insults as jokes
- Uses silent treatment or stonewalling to punish
- Does not take accountability for their bad behavior
- Blames things on you, other people, or the situation
- Has fantasies of grandeur
- Believes they are always right
- Gives themselves credit for everything and steals credit from others
- Can be very charming and friendly
- Can be extremely sexual and use sex as a punishment or reward
- Always plays the victim
- Is secretive, non-transparent, and vague
- Gives you the feeling that something isn't right about them that you can't put your finger on
- Boasts about lies they got away with

- Cheats
- Financially irresponsible and often in debt
- Makes you feel insecure when you spend more time with them
- Does not respect boundaries, rules, or authority
- Uses people for their own gain
- Expects others to do things for them but only does things for others when it benefits them
- Emotionally abusive, especially when they don't get their way
- Guilt-trips others to get their way
- Uses "love-bombing" to lure you into a relationship or to pull you back in if they feel you slipping away
- Often has addiction problems
- Insatiable
- Easily bored
- Projects their own insecurities onto you or others
- Gaslights you and others
- Uses triangulation to pit people against each other
- Makes you feel empty, unseen, unheard, and unimportant
- Very competitive and will try to win at all cost
- Provokes and then blames

**Fact: When we are unaware of the traits of a narcissist, we are more susceptible to a narcissist's abuse and can unknowingly be part of the problem.**

# The Symptoms of Narcissistic Abuse

*We teach others how to treat us.*

Sadly, many people who have been abused by narcissists will spend years unaware that they are being abused. The mind games narcissists play on their unsuspecting victims are designed to make them doubt their own reality. Having been manipulated and blamed for all the problems within the relationship, victims often seek therapy for symptoms listed below. A relationship with a narcissist can be detrimental to one's well-being. Too often, the target of a narcissist's abuse sacrifices their own health and happiness to please the narcissist, most often in the name of love. But remember, love does not hurt!

Targets of narcissistic abuse often feel:

- Confused
- Frustrated
- Anxious
- Depressed
- Overwhelmed
- Like they are walking on eggshells
- Sick
- Exhausted
- Fearful
- Shameful
- Rejected
- Angry
- Indecisive
- A need to be perfect
- Unlovable
- Unwanted
- Unimportant
- Insecure
- Lonely
- Stupid
- Crazy
- Paranoid
- Needy
- Unworthy
- Indecisive
- Misunderstood

**Fact: Narcissists are sore losers and will do anything to win.**

## Letting Go

"The journey of a thousand miles begins
with a single step."—Lao Tzu

I needed backup, a small army of support soldiers who
would stand behind me through the war that was about to
ensue. I disclosed everything to family and friends as I
began mourning the loss of my marriage. I soon realized
that the sadness I felt was not due to the loss of the
marriage but to the loss of what I wanted the marriage to
be. The difference was crucial to my grieving process.

I decided to cry as much as I needed to for as long as I
needed to. I cried in the shower, in the car, and on the back
of my Labrador retriever, may he rest in peace. He was a
real trooper, unlike my Lhasapoo, who I rescued 11 years
earlier when I saw her yelping and crying in a small pet
shop in New Jersey. Whenever my tears came, she ran away
and hid under the sofa. I swear she rolled her eyes at me a
few times as though she couldn't deal with the drama. But

my Lab shouldered every tear like a loyal, faithful companion, so I took full advantage, knowing that he was the only male on this planet who would suffer my waterworks for more than five minutes.

I wanted to get it all out of my system, so I continued to disclose most of what I had dealt with for 20 years to friends and family. On some level, I knew that the key to any future happiness relied on conjuring up the courage to verbalize it to others so that I couldn't take it back.

"You wanna know what's really weird?" I asked, sitting across from Mare at a local Chinese restaurant.

"What?" she asked, unwrapping a set of wooden utensils.

"I always dreaded the greeting card aisle." I used a napkin to absorb the tears that pooled up in my eyes again.

Mare glanced up from the Moo Goo Gai Pan that she chopsticked into her mouth like a pro. "What do you mean?" she asked.

I looked around the restaurant and noticed all the couples dining together, engrossed in conversation, seemingly enjoying each other's company.

"I could never buy a loving, husband card," I said. "No matter what the occasion, I always gave him funny cards because seeing love poems in print was like telling a huge lie. He was never my best friend nor my soul mate like so many greeting cards tout. Nor was he ever someone I could rely on or confide in. It was easier to *tell* him I loved him rather than seeing it in print or writing it. I guess I always felt it was a lie because how could I really love someone who treated me so badly? In my mind, if I told him I loved him verbally rather than in print, the words disappeared into the atmosphere without any trace of their existence." I picked up a straw, tore a small piece of wrapper off the top, and squished it down as far as it would go before removing it to create a paper worm that wiggled and grew larger beneath the drops of tears that I drenched it in. "I wanted to love him, but he wouldn't let me. It was like seeing the words *I love you* on paper made my lie tangible, which made me feel even worse. It doesn't matter how many times he lied to me over the years, I was *never* a liar, and I hate that I allowed him to turn me into one too." I stared at the saturated wrapper that lay in a small puddle beside my untouched bowl of udon noodles. "I'm probably not making any sense."

"You're making perfect sense," she said. "You haven't touched your food. You really should eat something."

"Trust me, I've touched plenty of food," I said, thinking of the jeans that I purposely left in plain sight on my dresser as a daily reminder of my commitment to become "me" again. But quite honestly, I wasn't even sure what "me" I was referring to. Was it the "me" who I was before I met him or the "me" who I wanted to become? Over the past 20 years, I had either lost my identity or never really had one. I was my kid's mom, my husband's wife, and our business's office manager. "Sharon" hadn't been around in a long time. I picked up the chopsticks, fumbled with them a bit, and clumsily attempted a noodle grab.

"So it was really bad, huh?" Mare asked. "I mean, he acted like a jerk sometimes, but I always thought he was joking and that he was probably a teddy bear at home. Why didn't you tell me how serious it was?" She watched as one slippery noodle after another fell from my chopstick grip, like the hundreds of stuffed animals I'd dropped from arcade claws over the years in futile attempts to win at a game designed to drive parents bankrupt.

"Mare, I couldn't admit it to myself, let alone anyone else," I said, shaking my head. I twirled the sticks round and round on the plate to form a mound of noodles much too large for my mouth. "I kept hoping that things would get better with time and that he would change. I feel so stupid." With one swift move, I lifted the chopsticks, opened wide, and managed to grasp one noodle between my lips before losing the rest to their point of origin. For the first time in a long time, I laughed because I actually found something funny.

"So what now?" Mare asked, as I sucked the lone noodle into my mouth.

"I have to get an attorney," I said, attempting another bumbling noodle grab. I twirled the noodles in my bowl and bit on the inside of my cheek while thinking. Another wave of fear and uncertainty settled into the pit of my stomach as I thought about the kids, the house, the finances, and all his promises. Once again, I lifted the chopsticks to my mouth and opened wide to another disappointment of a single noodle.

I pushed the bowl away and reached into my jacket pocket to wrap my hand around the crucifix that I carried every- where for strength as I anticipated the mountain I was about to climb. With all the signs and warnings, I should have prepared for this. Thinking about divorce was daunt- ing, and admitting my marriage was over was lifechanging. "And you know what else?" I asked, as I took the chopsticks out of the bowl, wiped them clean with a napkin, and held them up in front of me as a symbol of the day I vowed to figure "me" out. "If it's the last thing I do," I said, shoving them into my handbag as a token of my commitment to a new beginning, "I'm going to learn how to use these stupid chopsticks!"

**Fact: Narcissists will use your insecurities against you.**

## Pop Goes the Bubble

*There's a difference between giving up and starting over.*

In the months that followed, I felt empowered as Gloria Gaynor belted out the lyrics to "I Will Survive" over and over again in my head. I changed my ringtone to "Fighter" by Christina Aguilera and compiled a playlist of power songs that would encourage me on my road to single-dom.

I was in a stage of healing that I like to refer to as the "bubble." The bubble was an emotional state where I gained a false sense of well-being that felt amazing because I had thrown caution to the wind, took a leap of faith, and finally found the courage to untether myself from the source of all my pain. Hooray for me! I was on my way, emotionally stronger and ready to take on the fight ahead. Screw him and all of his abuse and false promises. Ridding our household of his toxicity could only be good for me and my children.

But my soon to be ex-husband did not make it easy because nothing is more enraging to a narcissist than realizing that they can no longer manipulate and control their main source of supply. When I refused his offer to hire a mediator instead of getting attorneys involved, I waged a war. How dare I not acquiesce.

"You don't get it, do you?" he threatened. "You don't deserve shit. I'll take it all. The house. The money. And the kids because they'll want nothing to do with a worthless, useless mother. But that's just the beginning," he said. "I'll make sure that everyone knows what a useless bitch you are. No one is going to want someone like you. I'll make sure of it. So I suggest that you and your dumb-ass attorney cooperate, or you'll be left homeless, penniless, and alone."

Once again, I was perplexed at how his moods varied day to day, from an innocent victim who would from ending my life to leaving me with nothing. Which one was it? Was he really capable of either? Regardless, how crazy was I for ever letting it get this far? What was wrong with me? Why had I tolerated his abuse for so long?

Thankfully, the fear and uncertainty that had kept me imprisoned for 20 years began to fuel my desire to once and for all be completely done. The court date couldn't come soon enough. The anticipation of moving on gave rise to an adrenaline rush that made it hard to sleep, so I found myself waking early and going to bed late.

I felt like I could tackle the world, but I decided to start with my closets that were overflowing with years of retail therapy I had indulged in on a regular basis. So much had to be done for the new life that awaited me. I was really making headway, getting rid of the old to make way for the new. But there was one thing I didn't see coming as I pulled down a box from the closet shelf that was filled with family pictures. With 20 years of memories sitting in my lap, I suppose it was inevitable.

POP!

I called the one person I was sure would understand. "Mom?" I said, barely able to speak.

"Hey, babe. How are you doing?"

"Good," I lied.

"Are you sure?"

"Uh-huh," I lied again.

"Where are you?"

"I'm home."

"Is everything okay? What are you doing?"

Your bubble can pop at any time, and there's no telling when or how big of a setback it will be. It's like expending all your physical and mental energy into climbing the side of an icy mountain without a pick, only to lose your footing and slide back down!

"I'm cleaning out my closet," I cried, as I sifted through the years. "I've been doing so good. Until now. What do I do with all these pictures? It's like one big lie!"

"Do you need me to come and stay with you for a little while?" she asked.

## Back in the Saddle—and Stirrups

*You can't stop the waves, but you can learn
how to surf.*

nd of a marriage or serious relationship can be a series
s and downs, highs and lows, and your bubble can pop at
me, but I began to notice that the further I got away
the marriage, the stronger I felt. Thankfully, his threats
lence were nothing more than threats, and his attorney
t eat my attorney for lunch as he said he would. As a
r of fact, my attorney fought for what I deserved. Assets
equally divided according to the law, and he did not fight
stody of our teen son. Children did not suit his lifestyle.
as never present as a father during our marriage so why
I he be after our divorce? That was a rhetorical question.

aughter left for college, and my son, who lived with me
me, thrived in our quiet house that was no longer filled
rguments, insults, vile words, and criticisms. Our

"No," I said, wiping my eyes as I stood and watched 20
years fall from my lap into a heaping pile on the floor. "I'll
be okay. I have to deal with this on my own."

The photos mocked everything I loved by reminding me of
everything I never had. I looked at the clock. It was late
afternoon, the kids would be home soon, and the day had
slipped away with little progress. The past few months had
been a whirlwind. I was doing everything right: eating
healthier, exercising, and organizing, organizing, organizing.
I had been in full prep mode, but it seemed in that one afternoon, for every step I had taken forward, I took 10 back.

"Ya know, honey, you can't rush the process," my mom
continued. "Everything's going to be alright. It just takes
time. You'll see. When I lost your father, I joined a support
group. I met some really great people, and it got me out of
the house. Have you ever thought about trying something
like that? You never know; it might do you some good."

I opened the refrigerator, stared at the unprepared food that
filled the shelves, and thought about what I could throw
together for dinner.

"Yea, maybe," I said, shrugging my shoulders as another
wave of tears swelled up in my eyes. "Mom, I gotta go. I'll
call you later. I love you." I hung up, stepped outside, and
walked to the edge of our property to the large sycamore
tree that over the years had lost some of its bountiful foliage.
It seemed that a part of it was slowly dying as the other part
flourished. I leaned against the trunk and stared up at the
house that we had built for our family, and I cried. Not just
any cry. It was the kind of cry that turned so ugly that I
would have to leave town if anyone ever witnessed it.

It didn't matter how many tears I had already shed. The cold, hard truth was that there was no turning back, and for the first time in my life I was going to be on my own. Alone.

The reality hit me like a ton of bricks. It was like opening the floodgates. "Is this it?" I sobbed. Looking up from where I stood, a small white cloud floated by and disappeared behind the tree canopy before reappearing on the other side. As it drifted across the sky, I watched how it changed formation from a roaring lion's head, to a soaring eagle, to an awesome handbag, like the one I had just seen in Nordstrom the week before.

But I digress. I adjusted my footing to adapt to the raised, gnarled roots beneath me as I waited for an answer that didn't come. So I asked again, rephrasing the question as though the Big Guy didn't understand me the first time. "Is this where I'm supposed to be?" I looked down at my bare ring finger. "I tried everything!" I yelled, hoping He was listening. There were more trees behind the sycamore and beyond them, vast farming fields. In the distance, housing developments spread like creeping thistle across the horizon. "I did the right thing, didn't I?" I gazed at the far-off houses and thought about the people who lived in them. I wondered what their stories were—if they were happy or sad or caught somewhere in between like me.

The answer didn't come that day like I wanted it to. The clouds didn't part to reveal a message, a hand didn't reach down from the heavens to give me a thumbs-up, and a voice didn't bellow from above to assure me that I was on the right path. But clearly, in the book of life, our chapter had come to a dismal end.

Jane meets Dick.

Jane and Dick get married and start a far

Dick is a prick.

Dick meets Suzy.

Dick likes Suzy.

And Suzy *loves* Dick.

They play together.

A lot.

Jane discovers Suzy.

And Sally.

And Ann.

Jane is done.

Run, Jane, run.

**Fact: We are the most susceptible to abuse when we lack self-love and ha boundaries.**

The
of u
any
from
of v
did
mat
were
for c
He v
wou

My
full
with

divorce was finalized, and after a long, hard climb, I felt like I was at the top of the mountain where the fog had lifted. I could see more clearly the mess that my life had become. It was *his* fault, entirely. He was an abuser, a liar and a cheater. Not me. I was better off and figuring it all out. At least, that's what I thought.

But midlife is certainly *not* the best time to go through a divorce. Hormones are running rampant, and all the stresses of the breakup are piled on top of all the stresses of peri-menopause. Hormone fluctuation is no joke, and the symptoms can wreak havoc on the body, physically, mentally, and emotionally. Because I would eventually be stepping back into the dating arena, I decided to be proactive, talk to my doctor, ask some questions, and get some answers.

"How's everything going, Sharon?" Dr. Martin asked as he pulled two rubber gloves out of a small box on the wall and slid his hands into them.

"Good," I lied, staring up at the fluorescent lights overhead while placing my feet into the sock-covered stirrups. The examination room was cool, and the small paper gown did nothing to combat the goosebumps that covered my naked body .

"Slide down a little, let your knees drop open, and relax," Dr. Martin said before inserting the steel instrument between my legs.

"Easy for you to say," I chuckled, took a deep breath, and held it while he used a long swab to perform a Pap smear. "So, tell me," I said, embarrassed by the question I was about to ask. "It's been so long since I even thought about this, but can I still get pregnant at this time in my life?"

Dr. Martin finished his exam and removed his gloves before responding. "Well," he said, stepping on the foot pedal of the trash can to dispose of them. "It's less likely, but absolutely." He finished and pulled the small paper sheet down to cover me.

"Okay, you can sit up," he said. "Everything looks fine."

"Great," I said.

Dr. Martin peered up over his glasses. "Any problems or concerns since I saw you last?" He stood and walked over to the open laptop on the counter.

"Uhhh, well, let's see," I said, holding the napkin-like sheet in place on my lap with one hand and supporting myself with the other while simultaneously lifting my feet out of the stirrups so that I could cross my legs to regain some dignity. But I failed miserably, and I suddenly realized the absurdity of trying to keep my middle-aged hoohaa under wraps from a man who was just eye-to-eye with my labia. I pulled my newest pair of drugstore reading glasses down from the top of my head and with keener vision noticed a small patch of hair on my right knee that I had missed while shaving in the shower that morning. "No problems here," I lied and switched my legs to cover the stubble. "No concerns that I can think of. I feel fine. I mean, I don't *always* feel fine. But no one feels fine *all* the time, right?" I looked at Dr. Martin, who hadn't looked up since I started talking. "I'm sure *you* don't feel good all the time either, do you?" His attention was still on the computer screen. "Or *do* you?" I continued with a feeling of uncertainty about where I was taking the

conversation. I should have stopped with "I feel fine," but
my thoughts were getting the best of me again, so I continued. "I suppose I *have* been feeling a tad more sluggish lately," I said, holding my thumb and index finger less than an
inch apart to indicate a mild amount of sluggishness
because I didn't want to be a complainer. "And," I reluctantly continued, still using my fingers to illustrate, "I may
be a teensy-weensy bit more emotional than usual. My
migraines, palpitations, and night sweats have gotten worse,
and I'm irritable, anxious, bloated, and itchy, but other
than that," I said, reeling it back in, "I'm fine...just fine."

I nodded to reassure myself, as much as him, of my "fine-
ness." I adjusted the napkin on my lap and smoothed out
the wrinkles like I was prepping for a fine meal. "Really," I
said, still nodding.

Dr. Martin finally looked up, and for a split second l thought
that, with all of his medical wisdom, he was going to give
me some antidote that would send me skipping out of his
office like Charlie did when he held the golden ticket to
Willie Wonka's Chocolate Factory.

"Well, that's all perfectly normal for your age," he said.

My age? Ouch. That one stung about as much as being
called "Ma'am" for the first time by the grocery store
bagger-boy when I was only 30 years old. As Dr. Martin
closed his laptop, I pondered when it all happened. How did
time slip away? It seemed like I went from a young, vibrant
Miss to an itchy, bitchy, divorced Ma'am whose ailments are
merely a symptom of my age. A part of me wanted to
blame my ex for sucking the life out of me for 20 years with
a vat of empty promises. But thankfully, with age comes
wisdom and the realization that blaming him for my prob-

lems would get me absolutely nowhere. Being middle-aged and single was definitely *not* part of my life's plan.

A chill rushed over me, so I wrapped the paper gown around myself tighter while trying not to disrupt the proper placement of the lap-napkin. All I needed from Dr. Martin was a little reassurance.

"I understand that my symptoms are hormone related, but at some point, this will all end, and I'll feel normal again, right?"

Dr. Martin offered a flat smile.

"Actually," I continued, "I could probably embrace this time of my life if I just knew that feeling like I want to jump out of my skin and run away as far as I can is temporary, ya know?"

Dr. Martin reached for the doorknob. "Everyone is different," he said, preparing to escape the gripe of yet another hormonal woman. "All of the symptoms you're describing can be expected and are perfectly normal during midlife."

"You guys have no idea what women have to deal with," I blurted out, "or what a mid-life crisis *really* is." I smiled to camouflage the irritation of his nonchalant dismissal, and to my dismay, I noticed that in trying to cover myself, I had fully unleashed my right breast through the large sleeve opening of the paper gown. In that moment, I was grateful for my age. The younger me would have been mortified, but luckily age ushers in a certain amount of shamelessness.

I suppose it was a good thing that Dr. Martin exited when he did. One more minute, and I would have welled up and confided in him that lately I could be moved to tears over anything and everything. The day before, it had been a laundry detergent commercial that showed a mom washing the grass stains out of her son's jeans. I went to bed teary-eyed over what *was* and what *will be* and then worried myself sick well into the early morning hours over horrible things that *could* happen! The what-ifs can be paralyzing!

It is my opinion that a well-trained female therapist who specializes in peri-menopause should be on staff during every gynecological exam after the age of 40. As I got dressed, I thought about something my mother had said: "Maybe you should start dating. It could be a lot of fun."

Dating was something I hadn't considered until then, but it had been a year since I ended my marriage, and I had shed enough tears to feel confident that I wouldn't drop my heartache into someone else's lap. I decided to take my mother's advice and step back into the dating world to try to have some fun. If there was one thing I knew for sure, after all the shit I had been through, I definitely deserved it!

**Fact: Narcissists will try to take revenge on their partners after a breakup by causing them emotional pain or making them feel guilty for leaving them.**

# Who's That Girl?

*Don't get caught up in what should have been. If it should have been, it would have been.*

"I'm thinking about changing my name," I said to Mare during our daily check-in. She hesitated.

"You are?" In Mare's voice, I could sometimes hear how carefully she chose her words when talking to me.

"Just a thought," I said, but it wasn't the first time I had contemplated a name change. In fifth grade, after watching Pinky Tuscadero's debut on *Happy Days*, I asked my mother if she would write a note to my teacher informing her that I would like to be called "Pinky." I don't recall any other circumstances surrounding my request, but I must have been suffering from a similar identity crisis. It didn't seem like a huge request, but regardless, my plea was promptly denied.

"Can I ask why you would want to do that?"

"Because everything in my life has been turned upside-down. I'm not who I was, and I don't know who I'm supposed to be either. I feel like I have to completely redefine myself, and a "new me" name is something I'm considering as part of the process."

"Okaaay?" Mare answered, dragging out her response until it turned into a question.

"I went to the mall for a new wardrobe and am on my way to the salon right now to get a "new me" haircut." Mare was unusually quiet, so I continued. "By any chance, do you know of any good tattoo artists?"

"Okay, that's it!" Mare blurted out, "As your friend, I'm begging you to hold off on the tattoo. In your state of mind, you might get something you'll really regret."

"My 'state of mind'?"

"Look, Shar, you're going through a difficult time, you may not be thinking so clearly, and…"

"You're right," I said before she finished. "I *am* going through a difficult time, and I would really appreciate your support."

"Of course, I support you."

"It's a different world out here, Mare, nothing like 20 years ago. I have to get my sexy back."

"I know, but be careful. You don't want to make any rash decisions," she said.

"Speaking of *rash* decisions: I got a Brazilian yesterday."

"You mean…"

"That's exactly what I mean."

"What? How was it?"

"You know how it feels when you pluck a nose hair?" Mare gasped on the other end of the phone. "Worse than that!"

"Oh my Gaaawd, you poor thing, thank you," she said.

"Why are you thanking me?"

"For giving me one good reason to stay married!"

**Fact: Narcissists are not capable of feeling guilty, and they feel no shame about lying if they think that it will get them what they want.**

## One Bad Apple, or Two, or Three

"Do the best you can until you know better.
Then, when you know better, do better."—
Maya Angelou

In the animal kingdom, females choose their mates based on genes. Good genes produce strong offspring that will survive and prosper. It is a formula well designed to ensure the continuation of a species.

Humans, on the other hand, are much more complex. Is it our similarities or our differences that draw us to our mates? If opposites attract, then the latter is true, but do the differences that pull us together ultimately tear us apart?

When my marriage ended, I thought that differences had played a role in the attraction and demise of my marriage, and one thing I was certain of is that I did *not* want to go down that road again. With that in mind, I made a conscious decision to look for the opposite of what I *thought* I was attracted to. Surely, such a major correction would bring me the loving, meaningful relationship that I desired. How hard could it be? After all, people do it all the time.

I had spent an entire year mourning my marriage, so after 20 years of being off the market, I was back on, only 20 years older, with wounds, I would come to learn, far deeper than I ever realized! During this phase, I started to think about the concept of finding "the one." That implication alone provoked enough anxiety to keep me up at night. "The one," suggests that there is *only* one. With billions of people in the world, I could have easily missed him. What if I was in the organic section making almond butter while he was picking out a porterhouse? If so, I demand a do-over!

It was time to devise a plan. My first order of business was to purchase the biggest, brightest, most powerful magnifying mirror on the market. Raise your hand if your morning ritual consists of looking into a magnifying mirror to check for unsightly facial hair that has sprouted overnight. Raise your other hand if you've ever caught sight of one that you missed in broad daylight, with others around, and no tweezers within a five-mile radius.

I wanted to reinvent myself, and obviously, the way to fix what's broken on the inside is to change the outside, right? If you answered yes, then you would also believe that putting a fresh coat of paint on a car with a broken engine will make it run better. Of course, that can't be further from the truth, but the new paint will make it look better for a while, maybe even increase its value as long as you don't expect to get anywhere. You get the idea.

I told myself that I had simply chosen the wrong apple, which just happened to be a *really* bad apple, so all I had to do was pick a good one! I painted a fairytale in my head of discovering true love and living happily ever after. Wow, was I clueless. But what made it so much worse is how clueless I was about being clueless!

As abusive as my husband was, he was *not* the problem. As dysfunctional as our marriage was, it was *not* the problem. Don't get me wrong, *he* was most definitely *a* problem, but he was not *the* problem. We're all familiar with the saying, "When you know better, you do better." Well, I did *not* know better. I was totally in the dark so I reached back into a heaping basket of apples and, with eyes wide shut, picked out another rotten one!

**Fact: Narcissists like to be in control, and they derive pleasure from giving or withdrawing sex or affection.**

## PART III
## Girl Gone Bad

# The Dating Game

"Vulnerability is not weakness. It is our greatest
measure of courage."—Brené Brown, PhD

I might have gone a little wild in this phase. I didn't date
much in my teen years, and I married young, so why not
make up for it? I had nothing to lose. I figured that since I
hadn't kissed many frogs, it was probably a good time to
start. How else was I going to find the prince charming I
was searching for and where was the Millionaire Match-
maker when I needed her?

The idea of online dating was definitely cringe-worthy, but
having built my life around a circle of married friends, it
seemed like the most efficient option. A combined effort of
coercion on the part of my family was the final push that I
needed to begin the dreaded task of making a profile.
There's nothing like an ego boost every now and then. If
nothing else, opening myself up to the world of online

dating gave me one thing that helped set me on the road to recovery: Options. Lots of options!

One morning, I drove up to the coffeeshop window and ordered a medium, black, as per the five-day detox that a friend of mine suggested to help with the crashing fatigue that seemed to hit me every afternoon. I prided myself on being a strong person and didn't want to admit that my lack of energy could have something to do with the fact that I was approaching menopause and had gone through a traumatic divorce that consisted of a seemingly never-ending barrage of verbal attacks and death threats. I mean, what's so bad about that? The thing about abuse is that it trickles in, day by day, and if you're not aware, you simply adjust to it.

It was raining, and I felt another migraine coming on. As I pulled out of the parking lot and onto the highway, the window fogged and blinded me to the road ahead. In a moment of panic, I secured the cup of steaming java between my legs, turned the defroster on, and with one hand on the steering wheel, used my other to pull a crumpled tissue from my jacket pocket to wipe the windshield. It was a risky move but one that was absolutely necessary. As I leaned forward and reached my arm over the dash, the car in front of me stopped suddenly. I slammed my foot on the brake, the cup shifted between my thighs, and a stream of scalding hot coffee squirt out of the sip-hole and landed in my lap.

On any other day, I would have blurted out some obscenities. But that day was different. I felt good. The new me was excited about my re-entry into the dating world, so the second degree burns that I was sure to suffer because of my donut-shop coffee addiction didn't seem quite as upsetting. My phone beeped. A text message notification. It was the guy from the dating site who I had talked to the night before. He wanted to say good morning, let me know that he enjoyed our conversation, and was hoping that we could get together soon. I replied, and we agreed on a time and place to meet. For the first time in years, the feeling in my stomach was nervous excitement, not dread or fear, and I was acutely aware of it. The "new me" ran to the mall for a new outfit, and with visions of "Mr. Right" dancing in my head, I let the dating games begin!

**Fact: Narcissists have little to no empathy and are not able to genuinely care for nor love you.**

# The False Advertiser

*The wrong people will always teach you the right lessons.*

It probably doesn't come as much of a surprise that my first date did *not* turn out as I had hoped. On his profile, he was attractive and interesting. When we talked on the phone, the conversation flowed, and I was hopeful. We made each other laugh, and the excitement began to grow. This could be him, "the one," finally. I delighted in the exuberant feeling of a blossoming romance. We agreed to meet at a public location in accordance with Online Dating 101. My expectations were high. Why wouldn't they be? He was everything I was looking for.

Handsome.

Witty.

Successful.

And to top it all off, he liked candlelight dinners for two and long walks on the beach! What could possibly go wrong?

We agreed on a restaurant near a local mall for dinner. I arrived in plenty of time and sat in my car for a few minutes, hoping to catch a glimpse of him before our official meet-up. As I walked to the door, I searched for the guy in the pictures, with the expressive eyes and warm smile. The guy who dressed nice, stayed in shape, and had it all going on. The one who was "the one."

I grew more nervous with each passing minute. I checked my phone. No calls. No texts. I opened the door and peeked inside. Still no sign of him, just a women sitting next to a guy with his head buried in a menu. *What if he doesn't show? How long should I wait? Did I buy this new outfit for nothing? And, oh my God, is Macy's having another one-day sale?* I started to sweat and hoped that others wouldn't notice my uneasiness. I fidgeted with my phone, checked some emails, and looked around again before hearing someone behind me say my name, *"Sharon?"*

I recognized his voice. It's him. He's here. Behind me. This is it. My heart raced as I turned to greet the love of my life. I'm a little unclear as to what happened in the following seconds. I either blacked out or was abducted by aliens and victim to some sort of weird, unexplained time-lapse that left me dazed and confused. It could have also been another episode of perimenopausal fogginess that temporarily seized all my mental awareness. Or maybe, just maybe, it was the shock of this guy looking *nothing like his pictures!* Whatever the case, when I came to, I was at an absolute loss for words. Even a simple "Hi" escaped me. This is *not* him. It couldn't be. So this is what fight or flight is all about, a split-second decision on whether or not to run in a moment of panic! Fleeing would be so rude, wouldn't it? Yes, of course it would. Silly question. But one that definitely had to be posed. I managed a "hello" as I shuffled through the rolodex in my mind of the dating-site pictures that drew me into his web. Suddenly, a strange sense of guilt set in. The angel on my shoulder was telling me I was being shallow, that he was probably a really great guy. But the devil on my other shoulder was pissed!

If a picture says a thousand words, this guy's picture told a thousand lies. They had to be at least 10 years old. He was a walking false-advertisement, and I had every right to walk away but I would never do that, so I learned a few valuable lessons that day that are arguably superficial, but valuable, nonetheless. Always insist on several current photos, full body, no hats or sunglasses. Don't commit to dinner when meeting for the first time because being in a position where you are forced to spend more than an hour with a complete stranger is far too much pressure. And no matter what you do, never, ever, plan to meet on a day when there is a big, one-day sale event going on at Macy's!

**Fact: Narcissists envy others and believe others envy them.**

# The Full Monty

*It is better to be alone than in bad company.*

After our date, the False Advertiser asked to get together again. While I definitely did not want to accept, saying no has always been difficult for me, so I stalled and told him that I would call him further into the week. Looking back, my inability to politely decline his invitation was a clear indicator that I had some work to do.

Over the next few days, he sent some texts and then an unrequested picture. A "pic" as we have come to know it. Not just any pic. A dick pic. Talk about having balls! Literally. What was this guy thinking? I was shocked and confused. I had to talk to Mare STAT!

"Sooo, remember that guy from the dating site I told you about?"

"Yeah," she said.

"I met him the other night."

"How'd it go?"

"Not well."

"Oh no? What happened?"

"You're not going to believe what he did."

"What?"

"He sent me a picture of himself."

"What's wrong with that?" she asked, sounding a little winded. I could tell that I had caught her in the middle of cleaning, which was not unusual. Her house was immaculate. The large, custom-built colonial was her dream home, everything she had ever wanted, furnished and decorated with period pieces that she shopped for around the country. She had made her home both a hobby and an accomplishment, and I was always amazed at how she managed to keep it in such order with four children running around.

"Well, it wasn't a picture of his entire self, it was a picture of his *entire* self, if you know what I mean," I said.

Mare's television was playing in the background, and the hesitation of her response indicated that her attention was being divided into thirds: her favorite morning show, housework, and her newly single friend who had been cast out into a world where she didn't belong.

"What do you mean?" she asked. "Hold on for a minute! There are Cheerios on the bathroom floor!" She turned on her dustbuster. "Jesus Christ, these kids are gonna be the death of me."

I pictured her pulling the small vacuum from a cleaning belt, like a cowboy in an old Western would draw a gun from his holster.

"I'm almost done!" she yelled above the hum of the motor. "Okay," she said and turned it off. "What were you saying?"

"He sent me a dick pic," I blurted out.

"A what?" She turned the television down and tuned in to the far more riveting "Shar Show."

"You heard me right. He sent me a picture of his penis."

"You've got to be kidding me."

"Nope," I said, trying to fight the green monster in me that envied the fact that the biggest challenge of her morning was the toasted oats on her bathroom floor while I wrestled with the after effects of my life being turned completely upside down. In hindsight, dating at that time in my life was nothing more than an unhealthy diversion from reality.

"His entire body?" she pressed on. "Or just his…"

"Actually, it was a picture from his neck down, full monty."

"No head?"

"Oh, there was a head," I answered. "Just not the one *you're* talking about."

"Oh my Gawd, why would he do that?"

"Your guess is as good as mine."

"Was it out of the blue?"

"No, Mare, I requested it for my collection," I said. "Of course, it was out of the blue!"

"And was it…um…you know," she said and cleared her throat. "At attention?"

"Well, I'm no connoisseur, but I'm assuming that there's really no other way to send one that would be beneficial."

Mare turned her dustbuster back on for a brief second to suck up another Cheerios.

"Soooo," she said, lowering her voice to a nearly inaudible tone, "Are you gonna show me?"

"I deleted it, Mare! Do you think I'm supposed to save it in my photos next to my kids' school pictures?"

"Yeah, yea," she said, "Of course, of course."

---

That first date was one of my worst. On the heels of that, I had several dates that were nice…just nice. Nothing more, nothing less. I had some rather interesting conversations with some rather interesting men that didn't amount to anything, but at least, I was off and running, swept up in an ego-boosting whirlwind that distracted me from the fact that this time of my life was *not* supposed to look like this. My family was supposed to be together, and I was supposed to be happy because I had played by all the rules. Not fair!

But life has a way of reminding us that things don't always turn out the way we want them to. Sometimes the feelings of loss and abandonment hit me so hard that I would retreat into my bedroom closet, shut the door, and sit in the comfort of the small space. It felt like the only place in the world that was safe.

Months passed before I began to notice how cluttered my closet had become once again. The retail therapy was piling up. Some clothes still had tags, and boxes of shoes sat unopened.

On one shelf was a pair of hip-hugger jeans that I purchased when they tried to bring bell-bottoms back. I remembered the day I bought them. I lied when I told myself that I was going to wear them. The truth is, I never liked them, but they represented the playful innocence of my younger years that I had lost and desperately wanted to regain. I put them on and stood in front of the mirror, laughing through the tears that fell. Twenty years had slipped by and it seemed that I was right back where I started. Alone. Decades of trying to make my marriage work had resulted in the very thing I feared the most: the loss of it.

I stared at a reflection I didn't recognize anymore. In the past, I had identified as a wife and mother. With my marriage dissolved and my children getting closer to leaving the nest, I felt worse than ever about where I was in life as I struggled to answer two very simple questions:

*"Who am I?"*

*"Why am I here?"*

Remember the basket of bad apples I mentioned? Well, this time, instead of reaching in with one hand, I tied both hands behind my back and dove in headfirst!

**Fact: Narcissists purposely twist any conversation to maintain control over the other person and deprive them of a voice.**

## The Wily Weeper

A boundary enforced keeps an abuser at bay.

I had been in the dating game for a couple of months when I started talking to a guy I met at the gym I belong to. He was an attorney whose wife had passed away several years earlier. He told me that he had taken the time he needed to mourn and that he was ready to date. But you know that little voice in your head that tells you something is wrong or not to do something? Well, as usual, I ignored it and entered into a relationship with him.

The truth is, neither one of us was ready. I was his life preserver, and he was mine. We got serious quickly, and within a year, we were planning on moving in together. He told me he loved me but made sure to regularly remind me of how much he loved his deceased wife and what a great marriage they had had. He teared up often when he spoke of her and asked me to watch their family videos while sitting in a room enshrined with photos of the "love of his life."

"You should feel special that I want to share my memories with you," he said.

But I didn't *feel* special. I felt *invisible*, again.

I couldn't breathe, and I couldn't complain. All I could do was try harder. As it turned out, our relationship was merely a continuation of my dysfunctional marriage and, in my opinion, a continuation of his as well. If I spoke up about anything that bothered me, I was punished. Only this time, it wasn't verbal assaults or threats. It was something I had never experienced before: the silent treatment.

"Sharon, Sharon," he would say, as though reprimanding a child. "I'm not talking about this. I'll call you later."

Days or weeks would pass before he would call and talk to me as though nothing had happened.

The problems in our relationship were never discussed or resolved. He wouldn't permit it. They were, as he would say, "put behind us," which meant conveniently brushed under the rug and dismissed. It took me more than a year to begin to push back. He had me so convinced that he was a good, caring man that his abusive behavior went under the radar and over my head. The **silent treatment** is a tactic used by an abuser to manipulate, dominate, and control.

From an abuser's standpoint, if they punish you when you push back, question them, or try to assert a boundary, then you simply won't try anymore. It worked on me every time. The fear of being ignored made me try even harder to gain his approval as I continually attempted to squeeze into a mold that he had created to suit *his* needs. In the process, once again I relinquished all my power and gave in to the martyrdom that he used to keep me in my place.

Our relationship ended abruptly when he called after a weeklong silent treatment and for the first time, I did not answer. I'm not certain if it was a sign of exhaustion, strength, or both, but either way, I decided that day to listen to the little voice inside of me that was telling me not to. That was all it took for him to disappear. I was sad and hurt.

His mistreatment opened and poured salt into all of the wounds of my marriage. I doubted everything I did, how I acted, and how I looked. I felt unimportant and unworthy, and despite his despicable behavior, I still struggled with my decision to ignore his last call. Did not answering mean that I, too, was playing the silent treatment game? After all my complaints about his punishing silence, was I now guilty of the same? I began questioning my intentions and my motive, stuck in a continuous loop of self-doubt and self-criticism that was paralyzing at times.

Back then, I couldn't recognize the significance of what I had done. But I do now: I drew a line in the sand that day that I had allowed him to arrogantly cross many times before. The difference that day was that I wasn't on the other side waiting to draw a new one. After decades of being brainwashed into thinking I had no right to set and enforce a boundary, I actually did without even knowing it, but I was still unhappy and had no idea of how to find peace and joy.

My mother always taught me to pick myself up by my bootstraps, so that's exactly what I did. I grabbed my bootstraps, held them tight, and jumped right back into a heaping pile of muck!

**Fact: Narcissists project their feelings of inadequacy onto others by shaming, blaming, and punishing them by using anger, fear, and guilt.**

## Stuck in the Muck

"Growth is painful. Change is painful. But nothing is as painful as staying stuck somewhere you don't belong."—Mandy Hale

Have you ever felt stuck? It is probably one of the worst feelings in the world. Whether it's a job, relationship, or other life situation, feeling stuck sucks! After decades of being in a controlling marriage and nearly two years of tiptoeing around the weeping widower, I was single again but had no idea how to manage my freedom. Every major decision, financial and otherwise, had been made for me whether I liked it or not. I never had a say in anything.

In hindsight, the anxiety I felt about my independence was one of the driving forces behind me entering into such a serious post-divorce relationship to begin with. The irony is that, regardless of whether I was in a relationship or not, I felt stuck beneath the weight of a ton of bricks that were too heavy to carry for even one more minute, but too scary to drop for fear of them crushing my feet! I needed to unload them one at a time, which seemed like an impossible feat on my own.

I desperately wanted someone to tell me what to do, when to do it, and how! But if I had waited for someone to come to my rescue, I'd still be sitting on the closet floor, staring at the Louis Vuitton tennis shoes and fur-lined Coach bag that my husband gave me after one of his last "business trips." A lot of gifts had come my way in those final years as he dipped his stick in employees and strippers from coast to coast. But the only gift I ever wanted was the one he never gave me: the truth.

My next revelations of being a midlife single were realizing that love is only a word without actions and behaviors that back it up and that I'd better learn how to be my own rescuer because no one is coming to save me.

With my divorce under my belt and a lesson learned from the toxic weeper, I took another step towards my independence by deciding to downsize. Next to leaving my marriage, it was the biggest decision I ever had to make on my own. My daughter would soon be leaving for college and my son's high school social life left my once bustling nest feeling empty. I sold our house, pawned off my ex-husband's meaningless gifts of guilt and bought a smaller home where my children and I could make new memories in a house that wasn't soiled by the past. It was a fresh start. I felt a little lighter and proud of myself for figuring out how to get rid of some of those bricks that were weighing me down. But the revelations kept coming as I entered into another relationship too soon and for all the wrong reasons.

"Hey, Mare, it's me."

"What's going on?" she asked. "How do you like your new place?"

"All is good here," I said. "I've settled in, but I miss seeing you every day."

Mare hung in there through it all, listening to my complaints and woes as I vacillated from happy one day to sad the next. I gotta give it to her, she listened to me even when I was sick of listening to myself.

"Soo…any new prospects on the horizon?" she asked.

"I've been seeing someone."

"Wow, that was fast!"

"Why wait? It's not like I'm getting any younger." It took less than a month for me to dive back into another relationship with the first person who actively pursued me.

"Don't you think that maybe you should have taken a breather before jumping back into the deep end?" she asked.

It was a good point that I would never admit to, but she had no idea what I was going through. I had a void in my life. An emptiness. A space that had to be filled to find the happiness that I desired. All I needed was "the one."

The good news is that I wasn't stuck anymore, but the bad news is that my life was moving at a speed that made it difficult to determine whether the path I was on was good or bad, right or wrong. It was like finally finding the strength to pull myself out of neck-high quicksand, only to trip and stumble down a hill, like a tire that falls off the back of a pickup and wobbles out of control until slamming into something.

"Well, how's it goin' so far?" Mare asked.

"It's okay."

"It's okaaay?" she said, dragging out the a. "That's not good."

"It's fine," I said.

"Fine?"

"Yea, it's comfortable."

"Oh my Gawd! *Comftable*?" Mare's Philly accent always grows stronger when she's being emphatic.

"Yea, comfortable."

"What, like a sofa?" she asked, and I laughed at her analogy.

"So how's Roxie?" I asked.

"You're changing the subject," she said, "But that's alright, message received." Mare was usually good at knowing when to let something go. "Roxie is a pain in my ass. The kids begged me to get her, and now I'm the only one who takes care of her. The little shit is so God-damned picky, she only eats specialty food that costs a small fortune. I'd get rid of her, but she's so freakin' cute…but don't tell anyone I said that." Mare is able to fit a lot of words into one breath, and I sometimes find myself taking deep breaths to compensate.

"Don't worry," I laughed. "Your secret is safe with me." But anyone who knows me well enough knows that I am not a good secret keeper. Honestly, if Mare's kids had come up to me and asked me point blank if she really disliked their dog as much as she said she did, I would have spilled the cold, hard truth: that all her complaining was merely a coverup for how attached she had become to that little ball of fur.

There's a fine line between a lie and a secret. Although my inability to keep secrets has become quite a joke in my family, I like to think of it as not being able to tell a lie. For example, I still haven't lived down the time that my older brothers asked me what my parents got them for Christmas. At the time, I was old enough to know Santa wasn't real and observant enough to figure out my mom's secret stashing place, but still young enough to be intimidated by older siblings who could dish out a mean foil ball fight or tickle attack. I was taught never to lie so when my brothers asked me if I knew of any gifts my parents bought them, I found myself stuck. Lying was wrong so I nodded and hoped they wouldn't ask for more information. When they pressed me further, I decided that dropping subtle hints could lead them to their desired outcome while saving me the guilt of spoiling my parent's gift.

"It begins with a cr…cr…," I said. With a baffled look on their faces, my brothers leaned in closer. "Cru…cru…," I continued. When I got to "cruc…" they yelled out "cruci-fix!" I nodded again and walked away, feeling rather satis-fied that I found a place in the middle where I didn't lie yet I didn't reveal my parent's secret because they guessed. In my mind, it was a win, win!

But as it turned out, being a bad liar sure didn't keep me from lying to myself and my partners about how I truly felt in relationships, so it's no surprise that the relationship that was "fine" and "comfortable" ended too. In hindsight, I should have taken Mare's advice and avoided any relationship until I fixed my "picker." Being a good "picker" is imperative to any long-lasting relationship, especially when it comes to romance. One of the biggest mistakes I've made is repeatedly being a "pick-ee," instead of a "pick-er." I was arguably one of the best "pickees" who ever existed, repeatedly adjusting and conforming to the most persistent "picker!" Entering each relationship, my main objective was to prove that I was right for my partner. Not once did I consider if my partner was right for me.

I succumbed and adapted to each pursuer like a moldable blob of putty. And even though I wasn't happy, I stayed in one unhealthy relationship after another out of some twisted sense of guilt and obligation. I was committed to staying stuck in the muck, no matter what, because I was determined to make what didn't work, work! I settled for what I got, like choking down an entire piece of mincemeat pie placed in front of me when what I wanted was cheesecake!

In hindsight, I was low-hanging fruit, desperate to believe in someone. What I didn't realize is that the "someone" I should have been believing in all along was *me*.

I concluded that my lack of success in the love department clearly indicated that I didn't know what I wanted or needed. Surely, dating more people would yield a clearer vision, so I spent a year playing the field. It seemed like the perfect solution. After all, if I couldn't find someone to love me the way I wanted to be loved, then I wouldn't let anyone close enough to love me at all.

But the truth is that I couldn't find someone to treat me the way I wanted to be treated because I wasn't treating my *self* the way I wanted to be treated. Throughout our lives, we are told to practice self-love, but how many of us have been shown how? Many of us come from parents who didn't *truly* love themselves either and so on and so on. These generational wounds can be passed down and affect our relationships for the rest of our lives if we aren't aware of the work that has to be done to heal them.

As we all know, life can be a real bitch, and that bitch will keep throwing salt in our wounds until they hurt so badly that we have no other choice but to clean them out so that they can heal. Life was not about to let me slip through the cracks without *really* understanding what self-love is all about, so what did life do? That bitch sent me someone who would open my eyes forever. As the saying goes, "The truth cannot be told, it has to be realized."

Well, what better way for life to teach me how to truly love ME than to send me another man who couldn't.

**Fact: Narcissists can use tears to manipulate and control others.**

## The Imperfect Ungentleman

"Sometimes when things are falling apart, they
may actually be falling into place."—J. Lynn

Did you ever see a nicely wrapped package with your name
on it? It draws you closer. With the wonderment of a child
on Christmas morning, you marvel at the crisp paper, neatly
creased around the edges, sealed with a matching satin
ribbon that has been crafted into an exquisite bow. Your
eyes widen with the thrill of knowing that it was chosen just
for you.

You reach for it, pick it up, and delight in the anticipation of
what's inside. Your senses are aroused, and your heart beats
a little faster. It appears to be a perfect gift, something
you've always wanted. You hold it for a moment and envi-
sion all that it will be. It's something wonderful and fulfilling,
you're sure of it. The suspense is exhilarating.

You tug at the ribbon until the satin bow unravels and falls
to the floor. You tear off the wrapping, slowly lift the top off

the box, and prepare yourself for the big reveal. You won't
be disappointed. After all of this, you can't be. You peek
inside and lean in closer to view every inch of…

An empty box.

You're baffled.

And confused.

You expected so much. You look again, rubbing your hand
along the inside in search of the magnificent something you
had hoped to find. You turn the box upside down and vigor-
ously shake it, but the box is still empty. Disappointment sets
in. Then anger. You were duped, and you wish that you had
never opened it because the hope of what it could have
been was far better than the *realization* of what it actually is.

After a year of casual dating, I met a perfect gentleman who
was kind, chivalrous, and attentive. He opened doors, pulled
out my chair, and helped me with my coat. He wined and
dined me, showered me with gifts and trips, and told me
that he loved me and that I was his "date of fate." We
entered into a committed relationship and, in a few months,
began discussing a future together.

He swept me off my feet in a whirlwind of romantic **idealization** that seemed too good to be true. Let me repeat
that. **It seemed too good to be true.** Because it was!
'Duped' is one of the best words to describe how we feel
when we realize that we are in a relationship with a narcissist. Narcissists are great actors. During the **love-bombing**
and/or **hoovering** phase, a **grandiose** narcissist might
use grand gestures or extreme overtures of love, attention,
and admiration to entice and excite their victim. To further
secure their target, they may display oscillating traits of a

**vulnerable** narcissist, such as personal tales of woe and victimhood to gain sympathy, nurturing, and caretaking.

Either way, his goal is to perform well enough and long enough to get the target of his abuse hooked on the relationship by keeping her in an endless pursuit of the person she fell in love with during the love-bomb phase.

It only took a few months for the "perfect gentleman's" true personality to begin to reveal itself. As I would discover, he wasn't a "*perfect*" or "*gentle*" man after all. The nontransparency, inconsistencies, and **stonewalling** began. If I questioned something, I was punished with a fit of **explosive anger** or the **silent treatment.** His whereabouts were often unknown, and any attempt at a normal conversation about his day was met with what is commonly known as **word salad** or **crazy-making communication,** where he doled out a lot of lip service that didn't add up.

Narcissists can talk a lot without saying anything, and getting from point A to point B is not part of their agenda. For their own selfish reasons, they want to take you from A to Z to H, then back to B. The only time a narcissist will grace you with something that resembles the truth is when he wants to get you off his trail of lies and deception.

To avoid answering a question, the "imperfect ungentleman" talked in circles, upside down, round and round, and took zero accountability for his actions. As I began questioning his behavior, the **devaluation** began. Devaluation tactics that narcissists use don't always look the same, but the intention is the same: to diminish your self-worth by sporadically saying and doing things that make you feel stupid, crazy, overly-sensitive, weak, unworthy, undesirable, unlovable, and not enough.

When devaluing is successful, you become easier to manipulate and less likely to leave the relationship, which creates the desired outcome for a narcissist: complete domination.

Conflicts with the imperfect ungentleman were never resolved, and according to him, they were all my fault.

"Can't you find a different way of telling me what's bothering you?" he'd say, as though there were some magic words in the English language that I hadn't discovered yet that would be the key to opening up the honest-communication chamber of his brain. But the truth is that narcissists don't want peace and/or harmony in their lives. They thrive on chaos and drama and want nothing more than to keep us jumping through moving hoops of fire. As time passed, I became acutely aware that the only way to move forward in the relationship was to disregard his lies, deceptions, inconsistencies, anger outbursts, and silent treatments, while trying to figure out the right words to say and how to say them to make him understand what I was saying about how I was feeling!!!

*What??!!*

Now *that's* crazy! You might have to read that last sentence again to even begin to understand the frustration that one feels when trying to have a healthy relationship with a narcissist. It's like attempting to lasso a tornado—extremely dangerous and impossible. He never wanted a *real* relationship as he claimed. Healthy relationships require honesty and open communication, none of which he would deliver.

It became clear to me that my only purpose in the relationship was to meet *his* needs. My needs were irrelevant, and any attempt at discussing them were met with dismissal, rage, or silence. The old, familiar feelings of being unheard, unseen, misunderstood, unimportant, and not enough rose to the surface with the realization that I was living, once again, on nothing but **breadcrumbs** of love and respect. It was during the relationship with the imperfect ungentleman that I had one of my most significant midlife and single revelations of all.

I noticed something.

A pattern.

It was like I had purchased another brand-new record that skipped at the same point as the last one that I bought, and the one before that, and so on. I talked to my therapist about trying a new approach. "Diane, I've been coming here on and off for the past 13 years, complaining about my relationships, pointing the finger at everyone else. I know my complaints are valid, but I think I should start focusing on me and why at this age I'm complaining about the same thing I was complaining about when I was 22. *I'm* the common denominator!"

She jotted something down on her notepad and peered over the readers that rested on the tip of her nose. "I think we should examine that," she said and scheduled a session for the following week.

But after much consideration, I decided that because *I* was the one to bring it to *her* attention, I'd probably be better off figuring this one out on my own. That pivotal moment redirected my focus and kickstarted my healing journey.

I realized that I needed all the bad apples in my life to learn, grow, and heal. For the first time ever, I started questioning *my* role in each relationship rather than blaming those I was with. I turned the spotlight on me, sat in the hot seat, and began cleaning out my mental closet.

I found my headspace to be overstuffed with things I should have thrown out a long time ago but for one reason or another had chosen to hang on to, like the leopard mini-skirt I bought right after my divorce while I was going through my "I'm bringing sexy back" phase. But after a few years of looking at it, tags still on, I made an executive decision to donate it and a few other post-divorce impulse buys to someone who would actually wear them.

It felt good to have extra room in my closet. As a matter of fact, it felt so good that I moved on to my drawers and the bins of shoes that hadn't been touched in years.

Obviously, clearing out our mental clutter is a far more diffi-cult task that requires a great deal of time and effort. It's not easy, and some items are easier to let go of than others, but I was committed to living clutter free. I still am. I knew I'd have to dive deep to figure some things out. I had work to do and questions that needed to be *honestly* answered.

*Am I afraid to be alone, am I afraid of being lonely, or both?*

*If so, why?*

*What is the difference between alone and lonely?*

*Is fear keeping me in unhealthy relationships?*

In my marriage and other intimate relationships, I felt alone and lonely, yet I stayed because I didn't want to be alone and lonely! *What?!* I examined that further and discovered that my fear was also tied in with a fear of failing. In my mind, every relationship that ended was a failure, which led me to another question.

*Does the end of a relationship mean that it was not successful?*

In the past I would have answered yes, but what if I changed the narrative by changing my perspective? Could I then look at each relationship differently? What if I made a conscious effort to put my ego in the backseat instead of the driver's seat? Could I then, for my own good, determine what I learned in each relationship so that I could use it as a guiding tool for growth? Isn't that, ultimately, why we are here: to learn, grow, and evolve?

Life is a series of lessons, and the people who enter our lives do so to teach us. If we don't learn our lesson from the first teacher, life will keep sending us another one until we do.

**Fact: Narcissists get bored easily. You will always feel like you are trying to entertain them and keep them interested.**

# Eureka!

*Sometimes you have to go back in order to go forward.*

When I was five years old, I flushed my invisible friend, Sally, down the toilet. She must have been getting on my nerves, and I decided that I had put up with her long enough. After much thought and consideration, I disposed of her with one quick pull on the toilet handle. "Whoosh." Just like that, she was gone. True story.

Obviously, my boundaries were strong then, but unfortunately, life experiences can diminish our self-worth, lower our standards, and raise our tolerance for mistreatment without us even knowing it! On my healing path, I had to look closely at my family of origin, ask myself some difficult questions, and answer them honestly, without guilt, fear, or self-judgment.

*As a child:*

*Did I feel seen and heard?*

*Did I feel safe and secure?*

*Did I feel supported and nurtured?*

*Did I feel loved and respected?*

Despite the loss and challenges in the years that led up to my father's death when I was a teenager, I answered yes to them all. But the next question had more to do with what happened before my father's terminal diagnosis. It was a question I never thought about before that led me to a connection I never made before, which tipped that proverbial can of worms that I had opened up and spilled it out all over my lap.

*Growing up, what was my model of love?*

As children, we can't objectively see our parents/caregivers flaws and imperfections, and we certainly can't see the wounds that they carry from their own childhood, but what we can see is how they behave with one another. We can see if they are loving, kind, nurturing, respectful, polite, compassionate, and understanding, or if they are agitated, impatient, absent, indifferent, manipulative, and controlling. We can also recognize the roles that they play within the relationship, if there is an imbalance of power, and if one always concedes to the other.

The actions and behaviors of our parents and caregivers during our formative years teach us what love looks like. The unfortunate truth is that, through no fault of their own, parents can unknowingly hand down unhealed wounds from *their* childhood. Obviously, how they treat us matters, but what also matters is how they treat each other.

As I learned more about my parents' relationship dynamic prior to my father's illness, the problems I noticed throughout my own relationships began to make sense. The similarities could not be ignored, which led me to more questions.

*Was the relationship dynamic between my parents unbalanced?*

*Did my parents treat each other with love, respect, and loyalty?*

*Did I learn from my parents relationship that I have to please, appease, capitulate, and serve to be loved?*

*Do I believe that I need the acceptance, approval, and validation of my spouse/partner to feel worthy and enough?*

*Was it engrained in me to put my spouse/partner's wants and needs before my own?*

*Did I learn from my parents that I should tolerate and accept mistreatment, manipulation, and control?*

*Am I codependent?*

*Is my codependency a learned behavior that stems from the faulty beliefs of unhealed generational wounds?*

The answers to *these* questions were much more complex, and my eyes began to open to the familial dysfunction of generations that preceded me. Childhood traumas such as physical and/or psychological abuse can affect how we show up in our adult relationships. If, as a child, we felt unseen, unheard, unworthy, unloved, and not enough, in adulthood we might be drawn to people who make us feel the same. It seems counterintuitive, but when our childhood wounds are not healed, we can, on a subconscious level, continually seek the love, acceptance, and approval that we didn't receive as children from other people who won't give it.

In other words, we can unknowingly be drawn to relationships that foster the same beliefs we had as a child: that we have to do better, try harder, give more, and love more to gain the love and attention that we innately crave. It is our brain's ongoing attempt to be successful at what we couldn't achieve as children. Interestingly, the way our parents relate to each other, based on their own childhood experiences, is highly impactful as well because we might subconsciously replicate their actions, behaviors, and relationship roles that they patterned to us as love.

After gathering more information, it became evident that my relationships with men paralleled my mother's relationship with my father. Eureka! The awareness of how our childhood affects us can be a springboard to breaking the pattern of abusive relationships that might repeatedly show up in our lives. We've all heard that love heals all, but no amount of love can change someone who does not want to change. Repeated attempts to do so will prove ineffective and self-destructive, like trying to quench your thirst by drinking from an empty glass.

The imperfect ungentleman and I broke up soon after a cocktail party that we attended with a few of his friends. With drinks in hand, we made small talk around an impressive charcuterie table. I would have rethought placing a whole piece of melba toast in my mouth had I known that the woman next to me was going to lean in and pop the question.

"So," she whispered, for my ears only, "Do you two have any plans for marriage?" She raised her eyebrows and widened her eyes in anticipation of my response. Her question caught me off guard and at a loss for words. I turned to the imperfect ungentleman, who was actively engaged in another conversation.

To others in the room, he was a conversationalist, the life of the party, charming, witty, and generous. But to me, he was like a robot that turned on when his image was at stake and shut down or malfunctioned behind closed doors when there was no one else left in the room to impress.

As I munched and crunched on the crisp, dry cracker, I knew I couldn't play the game anymore. I couldn't pretend we were happy, and I couldn't deny everything I was feeling. I wanted to explode in a fit of truths and tell her and the rest of his friends what I knew about him. I wanted them to know how he *really* treated me when he wasn't pulling out my chair or helping me with my coat in front of everyone.

I wanted them to know about his anger outbursts, silent treatments, inconsistencies, and gaslighting. I wanted them to know that he is a liar and not the man that he pretends to be. I wanted to expose him and let them know that he is an actor whose public image is a facade and that dipping his finger in holy water and kneeling before a cross is nothing more than an act—and a sickening display of hypocrisy. I wanted them to know that whether he is playing the hero or the victim, everything he does and says is for the sole purpose of drawing attention to himself by gaining adoration or sympathy from others.

I wanted to scream, "He's a narcissist!" but thankfully my glass of wine was empty so I couldn't wash down the melba toast that had crumbled into a mound of sawdust in my mouth. There must have been an angel on my shoulder that night because unleashing the rant that was lodged in my throat behind the ball of breadcrumbs would have yielded nothing more than a cloud of crumb-dust and an unhinged spectacle that he could have used to bolster and legitimize a **smear campaign** about what a crazy lunatic I was! While his friend waited for my answer, I struggled to gather enough saliva to swallow.

"Um..uh…I…um…he…uh…"

"You don't have to answer that," she said, "I mean, why fix something if it isn't broken, right?" She smiled and excused herself to the ladies room.

Regardless of how many people surrounded me, I never felt more alone because it *was* broken. *We* were broken, badly, and like Humpty Dumpty, we couldn't be put back together. Not then. Not ever. I didn't fully realize it until that very moment.

As conversation continued around the beautiful display of cubed cheeses, I knew I was done…done talking, done trying, done explaining, done defending, and done hoping that a man who promised me so much and delivered so little could ever really change.

**Fact: Narcissists have a blend of entitlement, insecurity, and envious natures that often results in aggressive, vindictive actions, and mood swings.**

## Another One Bites the Dust

*If you want to heal, step away from things and people that deepen your wounds.*

My next revelation as a midlife single was learning that to practice self-love, I must be willing to walk away from what is not serving me to make room for what will. Putting *my* wants and needs last does nothing more than teach others how to put my wants and needs last too.

"Another one bites the dust," I said to Mare as we picked out a nail color for our monthly mani/pedi date.

"What happened?" she asked. "I thought you guys were really trying to make it work."

As I reached for the same shade of pink that I had chosen for the past few years, she opened a bottle of Big Apple Red and painted a nail.

"We should have had a contract," I said, waiting for her to settle on a new shade. She took a bottle of Galaxy Blue off the shelf, painted her index finger, and held her hand out to gaze at it from a distance.

"A contract?" she asked and gave me a strange looking glance out of the corner of her eye.

"Yep. A deal-breaker contract. Think about it: It would make things so much easier."

Mare tilted her head and squinted her eyes the way she does when she's thinking.

"How so?"

"When entering into a relationship, both parties have to agree to and sign off on a clearly written contract of basic relationship rules," I said, clutching the Precious Pink polish in the palm of my hand.

"Not for nothin', Shar, but it sounds cold and impersonal," she said, reaching for another shade.

Before I finished describing how the deal-breaker contract would work, Mare was on her fifth color and final nail. "This is a pretty color," she said, holding her coral-colored thumbnail up for me to see. "You should try it. It suits you." She laughed and handed me the bottle that read "A Good Man-Darin is Hard to Find."

"I'm glad you're finding humor in my suffering," I said. "Now, about the contract. Hear me out."

Mare settled on the red that she had started with, and we walked to the pedicure chairs in the back of the salon.

I continued, "If a rule is broken by one of the parties, the opposite party presents the signed contract and gets to walk away without any further explanation or discussion."

She shook her head and gave me an eye roll before asking, "Sooooo, what are the rules?"

"Everything you would expect in a relationship," I said, easing my feet into the bath of hot water. "Like being honest, loyal, transparent, consistent, considerate, available, and respectful. The contract would be simple and nonnegotiable." I turned on the vibrating chair and eased back into the seat.

"Aaaand the penalty for breaking the contract would beeeee?" Mare expressed her ambivalence by dragging out her question as she paged through a gossip magazine.

"I haven't worked out all the details yet," I said, shaking in places I didn't know I had. "But what I do know is that if I had had a concise, mutually agreed upon, deal-breaker contract in every relationship, I could have saved myself a lot of time and aggravation trying to argue my point," I continued, as my voice trembled to the motion of the chair.

Mare shrugged her shoulders and looked up from the magazine. "Are you getting pink again?"

"What's wrong with pink?"

"Nothing, but you get the same pink every time. Do you really like it *that* much? Why don't you try something new?"

"I don't know. It's a nice color. Not too dull, not too bright. I'm used to it."

"But another color might work better for you. How will you know if you don't try something different?"

"Are we really talking about this right now?" I asked.

"All I'm saying is that if you step outside of your comfort zone a little, you might find another color that you like more."

Clearly Mare was not talking about nail color, and I hated to admit it, but she made a good point. Whether I was repeatedly choosing the same nail color or the same relationship, I was clearly stuck in a rut of familiarity. As we left the salon, I thought about what she said. I thought about it as I drove home, and I thought about it that night as I climbed into bed with my perfectly polished Precious Pink nails. Over the years, had I become comfortable with drama and chaos? Had I adjusted to being treated like my thoughts and feelings didn't matter? Had I become so accustomed to surviving on bread crumbs of love and attention that on a deeper level I truly believed that was all I deserved or was capable of receiving? If so, was I subconsciously and energetically drawn to the very type of person I wanted to avoid?

If "familiar" feels comfortable, and years of being in unhappy, unfulfilling relationships becomes "familiar," then it makes perfect sense. My next revelation as a midlife single was realizing that I could actually feel a distorted sense of comfort in the same toxic relationships that were making me miserable!

**Fact: Narcissists cannot tolerate feelings of shame, envy, nor helplessness, and they are hypersensitive to situations that trigger these emotions.**

# PART IV
## Girl Gone Glad

# Relationships Are Like a Bowl of Udon Noodles

"And suddenly you just know: It's time to start
something new and trust the magic of
beginnings." —Meister Eckhart

Whether the narcissist in your life is a spouse,
boyfriend/girlfriend, family member or friend, it is a continuous game of cat and mouse, and I was a mouse most of
my life, lured out of my safe mouse hole by soft, furry,
purring cats who used my empathy and trusting nature to
satisfy their own insatiable appetites. Narcissists delight in
chasing their targets, winning them over with a false image,
chewing them up, and spitting them out, only to repeat the
game all over again until *they* decide they're finished. If any
one word best describes a narcissist, it is *insatiable!*

Had I known even half of what I know today, I would not
have spent years scurrying around those fat cats who found
pleasure in enticing me with false promises before snaring

me with their razor-sharp claws. Okay, that's enough of my cat-and-mouse analogy.

It took me decades to realize that my relationship problems couldn't be solved by me trying harder or acquiescing more. What I know now is that I will never enter into a new relationship being the same person I was in the previous one. The heartache of each relationship has been painstakingly reshaped and reformed into well learned lessons.

It is no coincidence that life brings to us the very thing we fear the most. In an attempt to steer clear of what scares us, we spend countless hours and excessive amounts of energy dwelling on the very thing we're trying to avoid. In doing so, we draw it into our experience. Boy oh boy, was that a difficult concept for me to grasp. The only solution is to let go of the fear.

But how? The answer is *not* easy but quite simple, and we've all heard it before: Face the fear. It's obviously easier said than done, and make no mistake about it, tangible fears can be identified and conquered with less difficulty than intangible fears. For example, if I want to overcome a fear of flying, I can become educated on how planes fly and read statistics that prove how safe planes are. Once I have a better understanding of aviation, I can fly more often. The more I fly safely, the less fear takes over, and the more comfortable I feel stepping onto a plane. A similar course of action can be used for other tangible fears, such as small spaces, heights, and spiders.

However, intangible fears are much more complex. They exist in the psyche and can hold an inordinate amount of control over us if not realized and properly addressed. Becoming aware of my fear of not being enough has pushed the door wide open to a healing process that has brought me more self-acceptance than I ever expected.

The next "teacher" who entered my life was a powerful reminder. Our brief relationship reignited all the trust issues that I had been working so hard to heal. It seemed our relationship was off to a good start. We shared similar interests and activities and enjoyed our time together, but when he told me that I was "the one" a month into dating, I grew suspicious. When a week later, he claimed to love me, I was on high alert. Other instances followed that caused me to doubt his honesty. I didn't want to rush to judgment, so I gave him the benefit of the doubt while I took more time to discern whether or not the flags were real indicators of **love-bombing** and deception—or merely a projection of my past.

He continued professing his love for me while regularly reminding me of how trustworthy he was, and although I still wrestled with the guilt I felt for doubting his intentions, I couldn't ignore the warning signs or my instincts another minute. Calling him out on my suspicions meant risking being called insecure and paranoid as I had been accused of in the past. It was terrifying, but I started to ask more questions and dig a little. The more I dug, the dirtier he got, and my wound split open again. Not only did I find out that he had lied, but when I confronted him with proof, he tried to justify his lies with more lies. He dug a hole so deep that there was absolutely no getting out.

Once again, my initial gut feeling was spot on, but to my surprise, the all too familiar scenario didn't seem to open the wound quite as wide as it had in the past. As a matter of fact, with each passing lesson, the wound got smaller, from a gaping gash to a paper cut.

The noticeable difference was the shift in my emotions in the days and weeks that followed. In the past, I would have felt sad and despondent. I would have questioned my self-worth, blamed myself, and wondered what I could have done differently to prevent the betrayal. I would have played out everything that had happened over and over again to try and make sense of it all. Instead, I felt a sense of relief and acceptance like I had never felt before. We've all heard that everything happens for a reason, but for the first time, I actually found peace in that very powerful truth. Finally…growth!

I had to tell Mare. In honor of my breakthrough, I asked her to meet me for lunch at the same Chinese restaurant where I first confided in her all my marital woes.

"You look great," she said, peeling the wrapper off her chopsticks. "New man?" She raised an inquisitive eyebrow and waited for another juicy dating story.

"Nope," I paused and reached for my fork as the waiter placed a bowl of udon noodles in front of me.

"Well, what has you looking so exuberant? Did you get something done? Botox? Fillers? Come on, you can tell me."

"To be perfectly honest," I laughed. "A little bit of both, but that's *not* why I'm in such a good mood." I watched as she masterfully maneuvered her chopsticks into a mound of plated food to deliver a perfect rice-to-chicken ratio into her mouth.

"They're teachers, Mare. They've all been teachers!"

"What do you mean?"

"I feel better than ever because of what I've learned about my *self* because of *them!*"

"That's an interesting way of looking at it," she said.

"Interesting and powerful," I said, tapping my fork on the table to accentuate my point. "What I've learned is that it's all about perspective and shifting my focus. Each bad relationship actually made me better at loving and trusting my *self*, which made the anger and bitterness transform into a genuine gratitude that I haven't felt before. It's like it opened up this amazing space for me to be my best me. You know what I mean?"

Mare sipped her tea and nodded.

"And you know what else?" I said, searching through my phone. "I joined an outdoor adventure group this week. My first outing is tomorrow." I turned my phone so she could see the group's front-page picture of a woman jumping out of a plane.

"You're going skydiving?"

"No."

"But the woman in the picture is skydiving," she continued.

"Baby steps, Mare. I'm going zip-lining!"

"Aren't you afraid of heights and speed?" she asked.

"Yes, which is precisely my point. I'm facing my fear and stepping outside of my comfort zone." I held my hand out in front of her to display my newly manicured nails. "See? Portobello Plum!"

Mare laughed. "Good for you!"

I reached into my handbag and unwrapped the set of chopsticks that I kept as a token of the day I began taking my life back. Holding the two sticks in my hand felt awkward, but I used them anyway.

"Cheers," I said, holding them out to hers. I scooped up some noodles and carefully lifted the sticks to my mouth.

I guess you could say that relationships are like a bowl of udon noodles because a couple of the noodles remained, and those that were too slippery dropped away, so I simply let them go. Mare and I finished our meal without talking about my relationships or narcissism because for the first time in a long time, I didn't need to.

Most of my life, I felt like I was swimming against the tide, barely able to hold my head above water, but I never knew why. The revelations I've experienced being midlife and single helped me once and for all to figure out the answer. In the years I've spent researching narcissism and narcissistic abuse, it has become clear that I carried codependent traits I witnessed as a child into adulthood. I had no sense of who I was, what I liked, what I needed, or what I wanted. Lacking my own identity, I was an easy target for narcissists, who at their core, lacked the same. Both codependents and narcissists seek to find their self-worth in others.

However, the difference between the two lies in *how* they go about it. A codependent will do anything to gain acceptance and validation of others, in stark contrast to a narcissist who will go to any length to manipulate and control others. Regardless of their distinction, the basic principle of Law of Attraction, "like attracts like," applies, as both externally seek self-worth in the other, despite how malignant and destructive their relationship is.

A perfect recipe for disaster.

A match made in hell.

In the past few years, I have spoken with hundreds of victims of narcissistic abuse, who are seeking information, answers, and support. They all use the same words to describe their situation: heartbreaking, devastating, shocking, debilitating, horrific, detrimental, traumatic, gutwrenching, and the list goes on. In their own time, when they are ready to accept the unfortunate truth about narcissism and narcissistic abuse, they will all ask the same questions.

*How could this happen to me?*

*Did he ever really love me?*

*How could I have been so stupid?*

*Is it my fault?*

*What do I do now?*

*How do I get through a day?*

*How do I stop thinking about him?*

*How do I heal?*

*How long does healing take?*

*How do I move on?*

The above questions have very involved answers, with the exception of two. No one who has been abused by a narcissist is stupid, and it is in no way their fault. The abuse they have endured did not happen overnight. Neither does healing. Realizing that they have or still are playing a role in the dysfunction is necessary to begin the healing process. When they understand that their reaction to their abuser might actually be fueling the fire, they can learn how to change course and take their lives back.

Healing from narcissistic abuse is a process that requires time, patience, commitment, and action. It is a mountain they have to climb, a fire they have to walk through. There is no shortcut and no magic pill. Some will succeed, and others will return to their abusers.

Those who succeed will take the same steps to do so, yet each will have a unique journey. Albeit extremely difficult, their road to recovery will lead them all back to the same place: their true, authentic *self*. With the right guidance, they will establish the root cause of their problem by looking at their past. They will discover the benefits of journaling, mindfulness, meditation, and self-care. They will learn how to reprogram their minds by slowing down and observing their negative thoughts to replace them with new ones by using positive self-talk and affirmations. They will learn how to shift their focus back onto themselves by opening up to new thoughts, new interests, new conversations, new hobbies, and new people.

They will cry and scream, and sometimes they will feel like they have taken two steps forward and three steps back, but they will forge ahead because they are resilient and determined to survive. They will never be the same, and that's a good thing because, when all is said and done, they will be better and stronger. They will smile again, laugh again, and in time, they will forgive. But most importantly, one day they will be grateful for their journey because it has taught them how to truly trust and love themselves.

———

There's no telling what the future holds or if my wound will be picked at or opened again, but it doesn't matter because I am confident that I know how to heal it. And with *that* awareness, there is comfort and less avoidance, therefore, less fear.

The real epiphany is that all my relationships have been perfect in their own way because they helped me to uncover and heal wounds that I never knew I had. Each one has brought me one step closer to my authentic self and the innate instincts that guide me. I am thankful for every relationship and every partner's invaluable contribution to my life. Without them, I wouldn't be the seasoned me I am today—aware and enlightened.

If life is a journey, there is a destination point. But I think that the destination point is right here, right now. I don't have to wait for that special someone to be there at the journey's end to find my happy-ever-after because it can be found in each step along the way.

———

I step onto the narrow platform. The tips of my shoes protrude out over the edge, high above the trees and valley below. I gaze out at the mountains in the distance. At this height, looking down makes my legs shake and my stomach queasy.

I take a deep breath.

One final thought.

One final step.

And I fall.

Life is an endless learning experience filled with ups and downs, peaks and valleys. There are no guarantees, and there are exceptions to every rule. I keep my eyes open, sink into the harness that supports me, and soar through the sky, tethered to the zipline above me. With the wind in my hair, I spread my arms as my fear of heights begins to dissipate in the space behind me.

This time, it's not a dream. I'm wide awake, flying instead of falling. I guess you could say I've grown because for the first time in my life, I'm not wishing that anyone or anything in my past could have been any different.

Acceptance.

Pure and simple.

Sometimes a painful ending can lead to a beautiful beginning.

And for that, I am eternally grateful.

I am a Girl Gone Glad.

## THE BEGINNING!

## Terms and Definitions

**Attention addiction:** Saying and doing anything to receive good or bad attention. Narcissists need attention to compensate for a lack of confidence and self-esteem.

**Boundaries:** Limits and rules that we set for ourselves within a relationship.

**Blame-shifting:** When a narcissist, confronted about their lies and/or bad behavior, shifts the blame on to others or on to the target of their abuse to maintain their image and superiority as well as to remain in control.

**Bread-crumbing:** When a narcissist gives just enough time, love, and attention to keep their target interested and wanting more.

**Codependent:** Someone who needs the validation, approval, and acceptance of others to feel good about themselves. Codependents typically put their own wants and needs last while being excessively preoccupied with the wants and needs of others.

**Cognitive dissonance:** The state of holding two conflicting beliefs. As it pertains to narcissistic abuse, victims with cognitive dissonance suffer from confusion, guilt, indecisiveness, and self-doubt because of the inconsistencies between their abuser's words and behavior.

**Covert narcissist:** Internalizes their self-importance while hyper-focusing on their need for attention.

**Crazy-making communication:** When a narcissist talks in circles and uses speech patterns that skirt around a subject to avoid a conversation or direct question.

**Devaluation:** Part of the narcissistic abuse cycle when the narcissist degrades their target to make them feel worthless and inadequate so that they can gain control over them.

**Explosive anger:** A tactic used by a narcissist to intimidate and manage down the target of their abuse when they are confronting or calling them out on their bad behavior.

**False image:** The fake persona that narcissists present to others.

**Future faking:** An abuser's way of keeping the target of their abuse hooked on the hope of what will be.

**Gaslighting:** Manipulative tactics used by a narcissist to make someone doubt their own reality and feel crazy. A narcissist might say or do something and later deny it, or they might tell you that you said or did something that you never said or did!

**Grandiose narcissist:** A narcissist who exhibits overconfidence, impulsiveness, manipulative tendencies, and self-centeredness in a showy manner.

**Idealization:** Part of the narcissistic abuse cycle when the narcissist puts their target on a pedestal and makes them feel perfect.

**Intermittent reinforcement**: A pattern of cruel treatment used by a narcissist as a form of punishment, mixed in with random rewards and affection.

**Love-bombing:** Part of the abusive cycle where the abuser attempts to influence their victim by demonstrating acts of excessive attention and affection.

**Narcissism:** Personality traits that include thinking very highly of oneself, needing admiration and/or attention, believing that others are inferior, and lacking empathy for others.

**Narcissistic personality disorder:** A disorder in which a person has an over-inflated sense of self-importance and entitlement, a disregard for others' thoughts and feelings, and an inability to handle criticism.

**Narcissistic abuse:** A type of emotional and mental abuse where the abuser cares only about themselves and uses words and actions to manipulate the behavior of their victim. Narcissistic abuse can also include physical, sexual, and financial abuse.

**Overt narcissist:** A narcissist who is grandiose, attention-seeking, and entitled.

**Self-abandonment:** When we don't trust our own instincts and second-guess ourselves.

**Silent treatment:** A manipulative tactic used by a narcissist where they refuse to communicate at all.

**Smear campaign:** A method of damage control that the narcissist uses when they know that the target of their abuse is on to them. They might spread lies, deceptions, and rumors about the target to discredit them to friends and family.

**Stonewalling:** A manipulative tactic that a narcissist uses where they ignore or delay communication.

**Toxic enmeshment:** A situation where a person has no sense of self or clear identity of their own and often feels empty, needy, depressed, and unworthy because they have blurred, weak, or absent boundaries in a relationship.

**Trauma bond (Stockholm Syndrome):** A strong, emotional, and extremely unhealthy bond that is formed between a victim and their abuser due to the recurring, cyclical pattern of abuse, which consists of rewards and punishments, ups and downs, highs and lows.

**Vulnerable narcissist:** A form of narcissism character-ized by low self-esteem, feelings of insecurity, and a victim mentality.

**Word salad:** Nonsensical speech patterns used by a narcis-sist to confuse and manipulate.

# Acknowledgments

I would like to thank Lisa A. Romano for having the courage to stand in her truth and publicly share her personal journey of healing from narcissistic abuse. You opened my eyes and started me on my road to recovery.

Thank you to the members of NASAG, Narcissistic Abuse Survivor and Awareness Group. You trusted me with the most fragile parts of yourselves. Thank you for inspiring and motivating me with your personal stories and words of gratitude.

Thank you to Kate Santoro for teaching me what true friendship really means, for walking the walk along our healing path, and for always answering the call.

I would also like to thank the narcissistic exes in my life, whose mistreatment drove me to a realization of the self-love that I lacked. The lessons learned from each relationship has brought me closer to becoming my most authentic self and for that I am grateful.

Most of all, I would like to thank God for His bountiful blessings.

> *God grant me the serenity*
> *To accept the things I cannot change,*
> *The courage to change the things I can,*
> *And the wisdom to know the difference.*

# About the Author

Sharon Lee Villone grew up in a small town in New Jersey where, in her early teens, she discovered her love for writing as her father battled a terminal illness. She moved to Pennsylvania in her early twenties to raise a family, and in the early 2000s wrote a family living column for a local newspaper. In 2016, she released her first novel, *Harness the Storm*.

She still resides in Pennsylvania, where she is working on her next novel and runs a support group for narcissistic abuse survivors. She is a proud mom and gigi, narcissistic abuse support and recovery coach, listener, hugger, chewing gum addict, endless student of life and spirituality, and humble servant of God, who continually strives to practice gratitude for such a unique and glorious human experience.

Printed in the USA
CPSIA information can be obtained
at www.ICGtesting.com
LVHW051526191223
766904LV00027B/1481

9 781958 711576